PLEASE RETURN

HOUSING

TRAINING SECTION

SPEAK LIKE A PRO

SPEAK
——— Like a ———
PRO

In Business and Public Speaking

Margaret McAuliffe Bedrosian

JOHN WILEY & SONS, INC.

New York • Chichester • Brisbane • Toronto • Singapore

Publisher: Stephen Kippur
Editor: Katherine S. Bolster
Managing Editor: Andrew B. Hoffer
Editing, Design & Production: Chernow Editorial Services, Inc.

Library of Congress Cataloging-in-Publication Data
Bedrosian, Margaret McAuliffe, 1942-
    Speak like a pro.
    Bibliography: p.
    1. Public speaking. I. Title.
PN4121.B374 1987   808.5'1   86-15880
ISBN 0-471-84466-7
ISBN 0-471-84467-5 (pbk.)

Printed in the United States of America

86 87 10 9 8 7 6 5 4 3 2 1

This book is dedicated to:

Frank, who was the first
And before him,

Cornelius and Margaret Harte McAuliffe

Garabed and Takouhi Bedrosian

Four who dared.

Contents

Preface

William Henry Harrison, ninth President of the United States, may have died of public speaking. At his 1841 inauguration Harrison delivered the longest inaugural speech on record into the teeth of a raging blizzard. He caught pneumonia and died one month later. But he was neither the first nor the last to illustrate that mistakes in public speaking can be hazardous to your health.

In contrast, Lee Iacocca, Barbara Gardner Proctor, and Frank Perdue are all proof of the benefits of effective presentation. We respect these people for their accomplishments. Iacocca is champion of the Chrysler recovery and Chairman of the Statue of Liberty and Ellis Island Foundation. Proctor heads a prosperous and highly-visible Chicago advertising agency. Perdue parlayed an eastern shore chicken farm into an empire.

How did we come to even hear of them? They told us. Each translated successful performance in their field into a message the public could recognize and respect. They gained our ears, our eyes, and our response. Effective public speaking helped all three to gain visibility, income, power, profits and impact.

Were the Iacoccas, Proctors and Perdues born this way? Are such skills the purview of a chosen few? Of course not.

Consider Winston Churchill. Described by John F. Kennedy as the person who "mobilized the English language and sent it into battle," Churchill worked all his life to overcome handicaps and craft his presentation skills. His efforts eventually looked effortless. Instead of remembering him for the struggles he had in speaking, we remember best his precision and his passion. "The words of Winston Churchill," historian Arnold Toynbee said, "spelled the difference between defeat and survival not only of Britain, but of democracy everywhere."

The success of all these individuals is, in fact, due in no small part to their mastery of public speaking. Six hidden messages lie behind that success:

1. Effective public speakers win respect, visibility and recognition.

2. Effective public speakers earn raises, promotions and other financial benefits.

3. Effective public speakers build power, profit and success for themselves and their organizations.

4. Effective public speakers are strong and successful leaders, managers and executives.

5. Effective public speakers probably overcame fear and other barriers to develop their ability.

6. You can, too.

This book on painless public speaking does not promise an instant presentation or personality makeover. But it will guide you through some principles that make the process of developing speaking skills fairly easy over time. The book focuses on how to plan, prepare and present business speeches more comfortably and confidently. It will help you present your ideas more powerfully at meetings, in speeches . . . perhaps even on television. You will learn how to become your own speaking coach and how to continue improving throughout your life.

If this book has a single theme, it is that public speaking is more than an excruciating ritual. It can be the centerpiece of your personal and organizational promotion plan.

We will look at where and how to apply your skills in typical business settings to yield the greatest impact and results.

If You Want To:

INSURE that people listen to, remember and act on what you say

INCREASE visibility, profits, impact and income

COMMAND attention and respect in meetings, in sales and marketing situations, in business and social events

ASSESS your current skills, strengths, and areas for development

RECHANNEL stress into presentation energy

TAKE CHARGE instantly when speaking

ORGANIZE your presentation logically, powerfully and memorably

RESPOND appropriately to questions

STRENGTHEN and RELAX your voice

MAINTAIN focus under pressure

MARKET your ideas, products and services more effectively,

Then read on.

CHAPTER ONE

Speak, Persuade, Succeed!

Why Bother?

You stand, smile, and look out across rows of faces. You start to speak with control, command, power, persuasiveness, and just the right touch of humor. Your presentation gets the contract signed, the budget approved, the stock price boosted, the candidate elected, the measure passed, or the supporters and customers won over. Speaking spells success!

Think of the impact of one outstanding speaker. What if, on that steamy day 20 years ago, the late Martin Luther King, Jr., had looked out across that sea of upturned eyes and remarked, "Uh, you know, the other day I got to thinking . . ." instead of "I have a dream . . ."!

Such is the power of words and presentation. Of course, few of us are charismatic orators on a par with Dr. King, and few of us need to be. But we *can* aspire to speaking with control and power. We can use skills in public speaking to increase our visibility, impact, and profits.

Such skills can even save lives. Candy Lightner does this every time she mounts a podium. After her young daughter was killed by a drunk driver, Lightner's grief and anger led her to give up her usual activities to take action and found Mothers Against Drunk Driving. Never a public speaker before, she found her message springing out of her mouth and hitting its mark.

Martin Luther King, Jr., and Candy Lightner were motivated to speak by events and circumstances that warranted discussion. But it does not take a tragedy to instill passion and power. You can learn them. Why bother? Because learning to speak effectively in front of groups of people can profoundly improve your performance in just about every arena of life.

If your job demands that you speak in front of groups of people, if you occasionally find that discussions at meetings leave you tongue-tied, if your inability to express yourself clearly when speaking is interfering with goals in your career and personal life, then it is time to learn the skill of public speaking. Your first step is to deal with the foremost problem: fear.

First, Tackle the Fear

Do you feel a little queasy at just the *thought* of public speaking? You are not alone. In fact, you might be interested to learn that *The Book of Lists* puts fear of speaking in public at the top of the phobia list. Some people would rather eat live spiders than speak in front of a group!

Before you start tossing salt over your shoulder, take heart and remember this: Fears can be, and are, overcome all the time. The skills, strategies, and handy checklists in this book can help move you, painlessly, toward mastery instead of misery in front of audiences.

Perhaps you recognize the following progression of feelings:

1. This is a fate worse than death.

2. I would quit my job first.

3. I would do it if forced to.

4. It is OK in small groups.

5. Maybe I am getting good at this.

6. Maybe they will ask me to speak at the conference.

7. I think I will request a slot to speak at the conference.

8. I would fight somebody for a chance to get my ideas heard.

9. This is exhilarating. What power! I have always thought I had a lot to share.

To move you along toward that last, positive thought, it might be helpful to quantify your resistance and attraction to the idea of public speaking.

Your Speaking Resistance Scale

Begin by considering how you feel about reading this book. Rate your attitude on a scale of 0 to 10. Zero on this scale might, for example, apply to you if you accepted this book from a boss, friend, colleague, or teacher who said, "Here, you *need* this." You are talented and accomplished in your technical field. Other people need or want you to speak to clients or groups of people, but you hate the idea. You do not really want to change. You will keep reading this book just to prove that it will not work.

On the scale 5 might apply to you if you are interested in acquiring better speaking skills but are not sure how to develop them. You vacillate between "Wouldn't it be nice . . ." and "But it sounds like a lot of work." You realize that effective speaking skills could yield career and life benefits, but you do not want to embarrass yourself and experience those uncomfortable feelings. You keep reading this book, though, because you hope that it will contain some secrets that could make public speaking easy for you.

Give yourself a 10 on the scale if you are someone who has always wanted to feel the power of persuading groups, the power of the platform. You have looked longingly at the great educators, politicians, religious leaders, celebrities, marketers, and motivators. Your hand fits warmly around a microphone. You already speak well and comfortably, but you want to do even better. You are reading this book to pick up a few new tips. You are also hoping to find out how you might be able to coach colleagues, subordinates, or friends who puzzle you by their total resistance to public speaking. How could they *not* enjoy being in charge, being the focus of attention?

Based on the three examples given, rate yourself somewhere between 0 and 10. Circle your rating on the following line.

0   1   2   3   4   5   6   7   8   9   10

Ask yourself, are you satisfied where you are now, or are you reading this book with the hope of changing your number? If you plan to change, put an asterisk over your goal number. In other words, you may have given yourself a 3, but you would like to be a 6; circle the 3 and the 6, but put an asterisk over the 6.

Putting Your Resistance to Work for You

If the difference between your two numbers on the scale is only 1 to 3 points, your task will be fairly easy. If the difference is more than 5 points, your task will be tough, but achievable. Remember that resistance itself is a form of energy. If you have no feeling about speaking, not even a negative one, you will have no energy for improvement. The fact that you experience resistance shows potential energy which you can tap to make the effort to change.

Where does your resistance come from? Is it shyness, fear of failure, insecurity? Most business leaders are unwilling to admit to such emotions. Those feelings should have been left behind in high school! The truth is that *everyone* has these feelings in varying degrees from time to time. Be honest with yourself about the barriers you face, and you will overcome them more easily.

Here is a list of typical comments and concerns that reflect resistance. Which of these comments sounds like something you would feel?

I am afraid of forgetting where I am in the speech.
I am basically shy.
What if my throat goes dry?
I will probably draw a total blank up there.
Everyone will notice my weak voice.
I am sure they will hit me with hostile questions.
What if they talk the whole time I am speaking?
People will know I am not as confident as I seem.
They will feel sorry for me.

Do any of these sound familiar? If so, be pleased! You have a healthy level of resistance, and the gumption to resist can be turned into the urge to improve.

Productive Focus: Can Everybody Become a Speaking Success?

Yes, everyone can become a success at public speaking. It just depends on your definition of the word *success*. To

you, does success mean standing ovations? New contracts?
Perhaps political office or a promotion? Television coverage? Enacting legislation? Whatever the specifics of your
definition of success, you can consider yourself a successful speaker if you are able to look yourself in the mirror
every morning and honestly say:

> I am a skilled and capable person, using my talents and
> resources, including public speaking, in the successful sup-
> port of my personal, business, and community goals while
> experiencing challenge, accomplishment, and prosperity.

In fact, you may want to adapt this statement exactly to
your particular circumstances. For example,

> I am a skilled and capable person, using my talents and
> resources, including public speaking, to win over new cli-
> ents.

Copy your statement and post it somewhere to review
frequently. Yes, you may blush a few times at first (especially if someone overhears you), but this exercise will
help you focus on the definition and role of your speaking
success and its relationship to your goals.

Remember that perfectionism is the enemy of productivity. If you can do three reasonably comparable tasks 80
percent perfectly in the time it takes to do one task 100
percent perfectly (which is probably impossible anyway),
is it not worth lowering your standards a bit? You may
never become President of the United States, so you do not
have to be as good as Ronald Reagan at public speaking.
Remember, the best sales professional in the territory, the
most productive vice president, and the most successful
small business owner need to be good public speakers, but
they do not have to be perfect.

Clarity of Purpose:
Five Reasons for Speaking

First you should set clear, reachable goals. To begin, you need to establish why you are giving the speech. Basically, you give a speech for one of five reasons:

1. You want to practice or polish the skill.
2. Your job or role requires it.
3. You will get recognition or ego satisfaction.
4. You will get paid for it.
5. You want to promote an idea, product, or service.

Once you have identified your motive, you will know what the potential payoff for making that speech might be and you will be able to gauge success based on the appropriate outcome. Conversely, how would you be able to recognize your successes if you were unclear about your reason for speaking in the first place?

Suppose, for example, you decide beforehand that your motivation for making a particular speech is to practice or polish skills. The group is polite, and there is no whispering while you are speaking. However, you leave the session somehow feeling disappointed that you did not get lots of applause and that there were not many questions. This group did not even pay for your parking! You feel diminished. But if you remember your initial purpose, you assess the situation and think: "These people paid me with their time and attention, so I could practice new skills— and that was tremendously helpful to me. Maybe there were no questions because I covered everything, or maybe I did lose their attention toward the end. That is something for me to keep in mind for next time."

Regardless of your motive for making a speech, each presentation you make has one main advantage—you can

use it to gauge your success. Ask yourself these questions
after every speech:

- Did I learn something to make me more skillful in
  making presentations?
- Have I met my job or role responsibilities?
- Am I recognized, visible, satisfied?
- Did I earn my fee? Did the audience receive full
  value?
- Have I represented my idea, product, or service well?
  Are they buying or expressing interest?

Challenge Readiness Inventory

More than 100 business and professional leaders recently
surveyed for The Synergy Group business newsletter
named the following 16 challenges for today's well-
rounded business presenter. Although you need not excel
in all areas to succeed, the greater your versatility, the
better prepared you will be for success. You might want to
take this test to rate your own readiness for a challenge.

For the following 16 questions, rate your comfort level
for the given challenges, and circle the appropriate number (0 = totally uncomfortable, 10 = totally comfortable).
Then put an asterisk next to the number you would like to
reach in the future.

1. Present a complete and   0 1 2 3 4 5 6 7 8 9 10
   concise briefing or report
   at a staff meeting.
2. Present a proposal or   0 1 2 3 4 5 6 7 8 9 10
   sales talk with appropri-
   ate documentation to a
   client group.

3. Meet one on one with colleagues, supervisors, employees, clients, community representatives, or reporters.

0 1 2 3 4 5 6 7 8 9 10

4. Deliver a 5- to 10-minute all-purpose, amusing, and motivating talk to groups from 3 to 3000.

0 1 2 3 4 5 6 7 8 9 10

5. Deliver a 30- to 60-minute informative and persuasive talk to groups from 3 to 3000.

0 1 2 3 4 5 6 7 8 9 10

6. Present 12 minutes of legislative testimony on a timely, specific industrial issue.

0 1 2 3 4 5 6 7 8 9 10

7. Participate in a panel discussion on some current controversy.

0 1 2 3 4 5 6 7 8 9 10

8. Participate in a friendly television interview lasting up to 15 minutes.

0 1 2 3 4 5 6 7 8 9 10

9. Participate in an aggressive interview during a crisis.

0 1 2 3 4 5 6 7 8 9 10

10. Introduce a major luminary in your field to 6000 delegates at your international convention.

0 1 2 3 4 5 6 7 8 9 10

11. Present a prepared speech from a text that your boss, delayed in flight, was supposed to deliver.

0 1 2 3 4 5 6 7 8 9 10

12. Work with a speech writer to prepare and present a formal policy statement for your organization.　　0 1 2 3 4 5 6 7 8 9 10

13. Present a 1-minute television editorial on the benefits your industry brings to society.　　0 1 2 3 4 5 6 7 8 9 10

14. Write and deliver three to five humorous comments for a "roast" of a boss, colleague, or friend to celebrate his or her recent accomplishments.　　0 1 2 3 4 5 6 7 8 9 10

15. Participate in a lively question-and-answer session after one of your presentations.　　0 1 2 3 4 5 6 7 8 9 10

16. Prepare and present a 1- to 3-hour training session with appropriate material for people just entering your field.　　0 1 2 3 4 5 6 7 8 9 10

Now find the total of the numbers circled and the total of the numbers marked with an asterisk. Subtract the total of circled numbers from the total of starred numbers, and read about your score below.

A score of 0 to 20 is superb! You are close to your productive level of mastery in most areas. You may wish to keep reading to polish your skills and to pick up pointers on how to help other people develop.

A score of 20 to 40 is good. You are well on your way to

full flexibility. A small investment of your time and energy can pay off handsomely.

A score of 40 to 60 is average. You are sometimes at a disadvantage in a new presenting situation, but you recognize that you can overcome this handicap.

A score of 60+ is challenging. You have a major project in front of you, and one well worth the effort. Be sure to set small, achievable goals, work toward them regularly over time, and reward your successes along the way.

Becoming Your Own Speaking Coach

One-day public speaking classes can cost $400 or more per person. Private 1-day coaching sessions can cost $1200 and up. At such prices, few of us can afford such a luxury. However, much of what a coach does is to help you in these areas:

- To monitor progress and development
- To evaluate the outcome of your presentations based on your purpose
- To identify specific areas of weakness and strategies for improvement
- To collect and analyze models of skill and power

Why not become your own speaking coach? You are the only person present at every talk you give. You know your goals and objectives better than anyone else, and you understand the technical areas of your field. The hardest thing you will have to do is to develop some objectivity—for that is essential to coaching.

This is where audiotape and videotape come to the res-

cue. Educator Anne Atanosian recommends that you practice on tape as a part of routine speech preparation. Then
train yourself to tape your actual presentations as often as
possible. Wait at least 24 hours for your adrenaline to sub-
side, and then review the tapes.

Use evaluation criteria from this book, or adapt your
own. Collect your tapes and evaluation forms in one place
and occasionally review them. You will be encouraged to
see the progress you are making.

Here, in more detail, are four ways to coach yourself:

Monitor Progress and Development

In addition to using videotape or audiotape, create a checklist of the criteria most important to you. Then listen and
watch your target skills in each presentation. For instance,
your list of criteria might read:

- Voice quality
- Logic of sequence, organization
- Audience response
- Strength of conclusion
- Effectiveness at inspiring action

Go through your tape and evaluate each criterion sepa-
rately. This helps you avoid vague, unconstructive statements such as "This speech was great/awful." So your response to the above list might read:

- My voice was powerful and varied.
- My logical sequence was good, but I should have
  saved that most convincing point for the end.
- Audience involvement was minimal, which was appropriate here.
- I could have been more crisp at the end.
- I did a good job of stirring up the audience after the
  questions and answers. I think they will take action on
  this issue.

If you develop the ability to differentiate among all the elements you observe, you will gradually build the capacity to focus on growth in specific areas. It is tough to change something as subjective and ephemeral as "awful." It is much easier to work on such objective tasks as "I need to improve my logical sequence." Keep an eye on your long-term progress.

Evaluate Outcomes

You, as coach, must evaluate with a cold eye how well you achieved your purpose. The more specifically you have defined your purpose, the better you can evaluate your results. Here are a few examples:

Suppose your purpose was *to inform.* You talked about a new product. In the question-and-answer session, many people spoke. They called the product by name, and they remembered its key benefits and features.

Evaluation: You have successfully introduced information about this product.

Your purpose was *to entertain.* You told some jokes you heard on television. You observed that a few people laughed heartily. However, some yawned, and others laughed nervously. Two people actually left the room during the ethnic jokes.

Evaluation: You did not tell the jokes well, or the humor was not appropriate for this situation, or this particular humor was not appropriate.

Your purpose was *to persuade.* You talked about your department's budget request. You observed that people followed along on the handout material as you spoke. They asked probing questions. The challenges dwindled, and after a few amendments the budget passed.

Evaluation: Full success.

Your purpose was *to challenge.* You talked about problems and opportunities in the coming year. You observed that people leaned back in their chairs, some crossed their arms, others leaned over and made whispered comments to colleagues. At the end of your presentation, they walked out quietly.

Evaluation: You failed to overcome or redirect audience resistance.

Contrast that with a successful presentation *to challenge*. You talked about some rough times, challenges and opportunities coming up, and this group's important contribution in addressing them successfully. You observed that initially some people were yawning and others sat with their arms crossed. They gradually moved a bit forward in their chairs. They asked questions; a few people offered spontaneous statements of support. Group leaders outlined follow-up steps. The meeting closed with your statement of appreciation and unity, which they applauded.

Evaluation: You successfully harnessed audience energy to address this challenge.

Keep in mind that results must be evaluated and compared to your *original* goal, not a tangential goal that you identify along the way.

Identify Specific Areas of Weakness and Strategies for Improvement

The effective coach considers an event and comments both on what was there and on what was missing. If your presentation lacked energy, logic, sincerity, clarity, fire, or any other vital ingredient, the coach knows. So you, as coach, need to keep in mind a clear standard of excellence for different kinds of presentations. Consider the eight qualities of effective speakers and speeches discussed in Chapter 2 and the five purposes for speaking cited in Chapter 5. Then, based on your understanding of public speaking as a vital business tool, develop your standard and measure your own presentations against it. You must see clearly:

What is here that should not be? What is not here that should be?

Collect Models of Skill and Power

The coach knows other people who speak well. But no one person would be the perfect model for your style and range of purposes. Instead, make a "collection" of models appropriate to you.

Consider great presenters of the past and present. Look for skills and techniques in organizing and delivering information, in using voice as an instrument of persuasion, in selecting the perfect words to sell an idea, in using humor with just the right touch, in awakening energy in an audience, in delivering unpleasant information effectively, in involving the group, or in stirring the audience to action. Look for people skilled in each area you may wish to develop. Do not merely admire them—observe exactly what they do. If appropriate, express your admiration and ask how they developed their skills. Rare is the person who was born an effective speaker.

Even speakers you might first dismiss as ordinary or poor should be observed carefully until you discern something they are doing that you could learn from.

Naturally you will also watch excellent speakers as frequently as possible. After observing them, ask yourself this question: How might this particular skill or quality be adapted to match my own style and purpose? Add to this collection frequently. Make notes on the strengths of your models, and refresh yourself occasionally by reviewing those notes.

One rule of thumb is that the presentation you thought was good today should be slightly embarrassing to you a year from now. This indicates a good pace of incorporating new skills into your natural style!

Short-term monitoring is also effective. Many profes-

sionals set one specific skill goal to work on per month or
year. In each presentation they try to practice the skill a
few times so that it becomes a natural part of their reper-
toire. They review their tapes and draw renewed energy
from each success.

Here is an example of a skill progression for developing
ease with using humor. The speaker followed these steps,
focusing on only one at a time, to add one new element
every 2 months for a year. For that person it was a good
way to increase comfort and confidence in six humor skills.

1. In opening comments play with the initials of the
group being addressed. "Welcome to the National Association of Bankers meeting. Let us speculate for a moment
what those initials, NAB, really stand for . . ."

2. Insert a humorous quote to help illustrate a key idea.
"It will help you remember this idea if you think of H. L.
Mencken's comment . . ."

3. Adapt a story from *The Wall Street Journal* or another
business publication, and relate it to this group and topic.
"Speaking of creative solutions, we can applaud the San
Diego Zoo which recently . . ."

4. Select cartoons from newspapers and magazines. Secure permission for limited use, and make them into humorous overhead transparencies or slides to link key ideas.

5. Tell brief, true stories from real life that are humorous
and relate to your presentation. "This reminds me of the
story about my uncle, the canary, and the clerk at the dime
store . . ."

6. Tell brief, true stories from your own life that illustrate
lessons learned "the hard way." You succeed in the end
after some humorously foolish choices or conditions. "So I
never train people in time management without describing
the single worst instance of time management in my own
career . . ."

This speaker used goal setting for new skills and short-

and long-term monitoring to continue developing speaking ease and excellence.

Key Ideas

- Speaking = persuading = succeeding.
- To start developing better speaking skills, recognize your level of resistance.
- You can put that resistance to work for you.
- Your most productive focus is to define what success means to you.
- Your purpose is clearest when you have decided which of the five reasons you have for speaking.
- Today's successful speaker prepares for a variety of challenges.
- You can train yourself to become your own speaking coach.

CHAPTER TWO

Effectiveness and Excellence in Speaking

A Definition

When Chrysler chairman Lee Iacocca came to Washington, D.C., to pay back the last of the money that Congress had guaranteed for Chrysler, he was entitled to crow a little. Yet there were many in the Capitol who still rankled at the loan guarantee. So Iacocca took a middle course. He stood in front of a room packed with reporters, smiled a half smile, and when silence fell, announced: "At Chrysler we borrow money the old-fashioned way. We pay it back." He brought down the house. Why was that tone so appropriate? It was irreverent, ever so slightly mocking, yet light enough to erase offense the moment it was said.

This is an example of speaking effectiveness—easier to define than it is to achieve. Here is a definition:

> Definition: Speaking Effectiveness
>
> You are effective in speaking when you are the right person presenting the right message to the right audience at the right time and in the right manner to propel appropriate action.

The last four words are the key to this definition. The point of the presentation is *to propel appropriate action*— to make something happen, to move the audience members to take positive steps. All the planning for your presentation results from deciding what those positive steps

19

are and structuring each element of your talk to move the audience toward that result.

Suppose you want people to sign the contract, elect your nominee, approve the budget, operate by new regulations, call their congressional representative, expand their current thinking, protest the new construction, or salute the President. In each case you would gauge your effectiveness based on creating the results you want. This gauge is not absolute. If they do not sign today, you have not necessarily failed. As long as you are one step closer to achieving that result, you are propelling appropriate action.

In addition to this laserlike focus on the action you wish the listener to take, the speaking elements listed below are important. All the essential elements help match the right speaker, message, and style to the right audience and occasion.

Effective Speakers and Speeches

How does speaking effectiveness translate into action? In the survey just mentioned, top business and professional leaders ranked qualities of effective speakers and speeches for the Synergy Group business newsletter. They agreed on eight essential qualities. Here, in the order of importance assigned them by respondents, are those qualities. Speakers we appreciate are:

•*Believable*. These speakers match their messages. They show us that they sincerely believe in their message. Speakers lacking this quality seem contradictory. An example would be a respected nutritionist and health advocate appearing in ads for the "scotch and grapefruit" diet. If the speakers do not "live" their message, how can they persuade us?

•*Dynamic*. These speakers reach the audience through

lively voice, face, and gestures. Their vitality helps keep the audience alert and listening. Speakers lacking this quality seem boring. Someone with limp, passive posture and delivery leaves the audience wondering, "If the speaker cannot stay awake, why should we?"

•*Comfortable.* The ease and confidence with which the speaker steps to the lectern, looks out at the audience, and begins to speak help the audience to relax and listen. They know they are in capable hands. Someone lacking this quality disturbs the audience. The speaker's lack of ease can trigger one or more emotions:

Pity: "Look at this poor jerk."
Anger: "Do I have to sit here and listen to this?"
Caution: "What is wrong with this proposal that the speaker is not confident about it?"

•*Enthusiastic.* The energy of dynamic speakers is focused in a positive direction. Voice, face, and gestures reinforce the positive direction of the content. Both content and delivery show clearly what the speakers stand for. Speakers lacking this quality seem detached or uninterested. We wonder whether the material is unfamiliar to them or just something they do not wholeheartedly believe in.

•*Knowledgeable.* In addition to the specific information needed to present the speech, these speakers give the impression of having a depth of understanding and experience we can barely glimpse. They reassure us implicitly about the scope of their background. Speakers lacking this quality seem shallow. We feel as if we have just heard all the speaker knows about this topic. Why bother asking questions that might just embarrass the speaker?

•*Humorous When Appropriate.* Skilled speakers use humor, usually spontaneously, to relax the audience following events that are hard to ignore, such as a major news flash, a server who drops a tray of dishes, or a previous panelist who used up most of the time allowed for the session. Such events create tension. Humor helps restore balance. These speakers also use humor to reinforce presentation points. Speakers lacking this quality seem priggish. These are the speakers who dutifully remember to "start with three jokes." They deliver the jokes woodenly and then breathe an audible sign of relief at finally getting to the heart of the speech and not having to bother with humor again.

•*Skilled with Eye Contact.* These speakers use three types of eye contact—room quarter, scan, and hold. They prefer to speak from a brief outline or a few notes rather than from a full script or text. If forced to use a text, they still maintain eye contact at least half the time. Speakers without this quality seem to lack confidence or to be unprepared, because they are overly dependent on their text. Even when working without a text, they look down. They may be hoping the words will magically appear on the lectern.

•*Skilled in Voice Variety.* Respected speakers treat their voices as melodious instruments. This means that they protect their voices off stage and play to the appropriate capacity on stage. They use volume, pitch, intensity, breath, and silence to underline ideas. Speakers without voice control seem nervous, quiet, or squeaky. They may begin speaking in a high, quivering voice that lacks intensity and conviction. They later "warm up" and begin to talk more naturally, but in a monotone they mistakenly think sounds formal and professional.

Speeches we appreciate are:

•*Clear in Focus or Purpose.* Early in the speech the key points are introduced, the points unfold as previewed, and the closing proposes to the audience an action to take or a single idea to ponder. Speeches lacking this quality seem rambling and a waste of time.

•*Tailored to the Occasion or Group.* Material, language, technical information, and examples demonstrate an awareness of current issues and information of interest to the specific audience. Speeches lacking this quality seem "canned" or too general to be of interest.

•*Clearly and Logically Developed.* Key points of the speech unfold in a sequence based on time, importance, geography, or some other appropriate order. Speeches lacking this quality seem haphazard or jumpy. It is as if the speaker expected the audience to develop their own sense of design or logic. Few audiences will bother.

•*Appropriate in Length.* In good speeches key points are given the time they deserve. A speech can be effective in 3 minutes, 30 minutes, or 3 hours—as long as the audience can still listen productively and there are still important points to be made. Speeches lacking this quality either cheat or bore the audience. Are speakers filling time on the schedule because the coffee is not ready yet? Are they dragging it out because they do not know how to stop?

•*Memorable.* This speech blends general information with concrete illustrations and examples. Each main idea is vividly backed with facts, visual aids, anecdotes, or other supporting elements to help the audience remember and act on the information. Speeches lacking this cohesive quality seem overwhelming. It is as if the speaker were dumping loads of data with no time for the audience to absorb, reflect, and understand them all.

•*Understandable.* Complex, technical, or abstract material is presented through metaphors, examples, puzzles, anecdotes, models, props, or visual aids to help the audience grasp the ideas. Speeches lacking this quality seem overly formal or academic. It is as if the point of the presentation were to impress rather than to give usable, practical information.

•*Realistic in Scope.* This speech is not overly ambitious or incompatible with the group's mood. Audience reactions are predicted and prepared for. An appropriate response is planned. The speaker does not use a cheerleader opening in a tense time. The audience may be invited to ask questions. Overall, the speaker commands respect through responding to the audience's sensibilities. A speech lacking this quality seems pushy. It seems that the speaker is trying to railroad the audience into something they may oppose or resist on further thought. Few listeners are instant converts.

•*Challenging.* A stirring speech shows the audience how to cultivate the best within themselves. The speech paints a vision of a favorable future for the people and programs concerned. The speaker offers insights to help the audience share and participate in that challenge and vision. Speeches lacking this quality seem pointless, lackluster, and boring. Yawn . . . just the same old stuff people always hear that nobody really believes anyway.

The Speaking Skill Development Inventory

The above qualities give you some broad goals to aim for. But following is an even more practical and specific checklist designed to help you quantify your desire to be a polished speaker and to decide whether your current skill level is productively serving your goals. You may decide to refresh or renew specific skills once you have considered their important role in your success.

The following skills and strategies will help you present ideas powerfully. In the leftmost column ("Current"), rate yourself on your current level of comfort and confidence with the use of each skill. When you have completed your current skill inventory, fill in the next column ("Future") with the number indicating your desired future level for each skill. For both columns, select numbers from this scale:

4 = I am very comfortable and confident with this skill.

3 = I am usually comfortable and confident with this skill.

2 = I am sometimes uncomfortable at this skill, unsure of my ability.

1 = I need to develop this skill.

0 = I do not yet use or need this skill.

Before the Speech

CURRENT   FUTURE

_____   _____ Analyzing the audience

_____   _____ Developing focus and objectives

_____   _____ Organizing my material

_____   _____ Researching recent information

_____   _____ Developing appropriate examples, stories, applications

_____   _____ Writing the speech, starting from the bottom line

_____   _____ Selecting appropriate humor

_____   _____ Preparing visual aids or props

_____   _____ Practicing on audiotape or videotape

_____   _____ Writing an effective introduction

_____   _____ Preparing for likely questions

_____   _____ Checking all aspects of the room and equipment

During the Speech

CURRENT   FUTURE

———   ———   Using stress positively

———   ———   Appearing poised

———   ———   Opening powerfully

———   ———   Maintaining authoritative voice and rate
                                    of speaking

———   ———   Using appropriate gestures and stance

———   ———   Taking advantage of silence for thought
                                    or emphasis

———   ———   Using appropriate level of language

———   ———   Including humor

———   ———   Balancing your objectives with the
                                    audience's needs

———   ———   Maintaining eye contact for a full
                                    sentence

———   ———   Using visual aids smoothly to underline
                                    key points

———   ———   Gauging audience response throughout
                                    the speech

———   ———   Handling a hostile question or audience

———   ———   Providing handouts or other materials

———   ———   Recovering from difficulties (interrup-
                                    tion, fire drill, hall noises, etc.)

———   ———   Closing with memorable direction and
                                    impact

CURRENT   FUTURE

———————   ———————   Responding effectively to questions and answers

After the Speech

———————   ———————   Reviewing an audiotape or videotape of my presentation

———————   ———————   Noting my strengths and areas for development

———————   ———————   Inviting feedback from others

———————   ———————   Revising style and substance for greater future success

———————   ———————   TOTALS

Add the numbers in each column. (The highest possible total is 132.) Since the survey compares your current skill level with your desired future level, the actual total number is not especially important. What is important is the *difference* between the totals in the two columns. Obviously, the greater the difference, the greater the challenge before you. A difference of 10 points is not much. You may just need a bit of focus and polishing. A difference of more than 30 points, however, means you will have to work a bit to develop your presentation potential—and the change you will see will be pleasingly dramatic.

So far you have completed three checklists or surveys. In Chapter 1 you completed the speaking resistance scale and the challenge readiness inventory. They charted your interest, comfort, and confidence in facing the basic business speaking challenges. The speaking skill development inventory you just completed explored your current and desired future array of specific skills. After a brief

consideration of the examples and elements of speaking
excellence in operation, we will explore those skills in
greater depth.

Ingredients of Excellence

Let us take a look at some examples of speaking excellence
in operation. Some are easy to identify. People in the public eye are an obvious first choice. Publicity automatically
creates a certain fascination on the part of the audience.
Think of Katharine Hepburn, Ronald Reagan, Geraldine
Ferraro, and other public personalities. These people can
be excellent partly because their lives, their works, their
reputations, and the span of their accomplishments have
spoken for them long before they are introduced. They
must still perform to your high expectations, but you are
generous in taking their success for granted. This first
group of excellent speakers, then, includes those whose
lives have spoken so loudly and publicly that their
speeches are primarily an opportunity for the audience to
see them in person. Political motives or jealousy cause a
few audience members to hope for the failure of these
speakers, but the regard and respect of most of the crowd
cushion these luminaries and magnify their speaking success.

Another group of excellent speakers includes short-term
celebrities or single-issue stars. Ralph Nader, through his
zeal and commitment to public safety, is a single-issue excellent speaker. Barbara Gardner Proctor, best known for
her successful advertising firm in Chicago, has adopted the
theme that women are one of the most potentially productive "wasted natural resources" in the United States. In
today's celebrity-hungry culture, Mary Lou Retton's 1984
Olympic gold medal in gymnastics ironically also earns her

a niche in public speaking and a place as the first woman featured on the front of the Wheaties box.

A third category of speaking excellence is composed of promoters of great results, who are not necessarily the producers of these results. In the first two categories, the speakers are presenting ideas based on their personal success in producing results in their chosen field. This third category, however, includes those who study the successful doers (often those in categories 1 and 2), look for patterns in what they observe, and synthesize the information into forms that help the rest of us. Author Tom Peters is identified with the topic of corporate excellence (Thomas J. Peters and Robert H. Waterman, *In Search of Excellence*, Harper & Row, 1982). Charles Garfield focuses on performing up to the leaders in your field (Charles Garfield, *Peak Performance*, Warner Books, 1985). These researchers report to us in a way that satisfies our hunger for the secrets of success. They developed speaking excellence by reporting primarily on the direct experiences of others.

It is important to realize you can develop speaking excellence without being a celebrity. When you stride forward purposefully, address the audience with your eyes, present your ideas powerfully, and leave them with a commitment to action, you are building both the skill and the reputation for speaking excellence. The goal is to reach a point of practice and comfort so that none of it feels like work. This is the peak of speaking. This is the moment of effortless excellence, the moment when all the "right" things come together with ease. You can make this moment happen.

Key Ideas

- The first step toward seeking excellence is to maximize your effectiveness.
- Effective speakers have eight specific qualities.

- Effective speeches share eight characteristics.
- You improve effectiveness by taking inventory of your current skills, strengths, and areas needing development.
- Use the inventory to help you set specific skill goals.
- Move finally from effectiveness to excellence.

CHAPTER THREE

Self: Charting Your Characteristics

The SASS Formula:
Four Essential Elements

In the next four chapters, we discuss the four essential ingredients of every speech. You can remember them as SASS, which stands for:

- *Self*—Your natural style determines the kind of speaker you will be.
- *Audience*—They are the cocreators of your speech, your listeners, your challengers, your responders.
- *Substance*—This is the organization and content of your speech.
- *Style*—Style is the method of delivery you employ in a given presentation—and it will vary.

Arguments abound as to which of the last two elements is most important, but this is like arguing which side of a coin is more important, heads or tails. Unless you have made a bet, they are both critical. Neither would exist or have value without the other. Neither style nor substance alone delivers what an audience deserves. Their union does.

You and the audience are also like heads and tails of the same coin. You work together to create something of value with the time they have taken to listen and you have taken to speak.

Your first strength is your natural style and personality—your *self*—and this is our focus in this chapter. This style can be tailored, refined, or enhanced, but it will always come through. And it should. Your background and convictions strengthen the ideas you present, so accept your natural style as a base to work from.

Each of us has a blend of six style characteristics. We vary in proportion and intensity, but all of us have the ability to be *organized, detailed, logical, spontaneous, action-oriented,* and *intuitive.* Take a moment now to chart your characteristics, using the Style Characteristics Profile. Next to each of the following comments, record the appropriate number. On the first round, describe yourself as you are in your career, not necessarily just when you plan for a presentation. You may elect to do a second round to look at your noncareer style. In response to each statement, record one of these numbers:

$$5 = \text{usually}$$
$$4 = \text{often}$$
$$3 = \text{sometimes}$$
$$2 = \text{occasionally}$$
$$1 = \text{rarely}$$
$$0 = \text{never}$$

STYLE CHARACTERISTICS PROFILE

_____ 1. I deliberate long and hard over important decisions.

_____ 2. I like to receive and present information in a logical, sequential way.

_____ 3. I often step back to restore my view of the big picture.

_____ 4. I make decisions quickly and put my energy to work.

_____ 5. I am comfortable in a fluid situation with lots of changes occurring at once.

_____ 6. My work is organized and prepared as far in advance as possible.

_____ 7. As soon as I notice details, I begin to arrange them into patterns.

_____ 8. I prefer not to jump from A to K, but to touch all the steps in between.

_____ 9. I thrive on urgencies requiring me to think on my feet.

_____10. I do not make decisions if some of the information is missing.

_____11. I appreciate at least a week's notice before I have to give a speech.

_____12. I prefer to take action and be wrong sometimes rather than to wait until every last detail is ironed out.

Add your points on the following sets of questions and record here:

Questions 6 and 11 (organized) _____

Questions 1 and 10 (detailed) _____

Questions 2 and 8 (logical) _____

Questions 5 and 9 (spontaneous) _____

Questions 4 and 12 (action-oriented) _____

Questions 3 and 7 (intuitive) _____

Record your points on the circle next to the appropriate wedge. Chart a point on the number line to show the point total for that dimension. Connect the points for a profile of your style intensities. Note your two highest and two lowest points. As you read these descriptions, recognize your

CHARTING YOUR CHARACTERISTICS

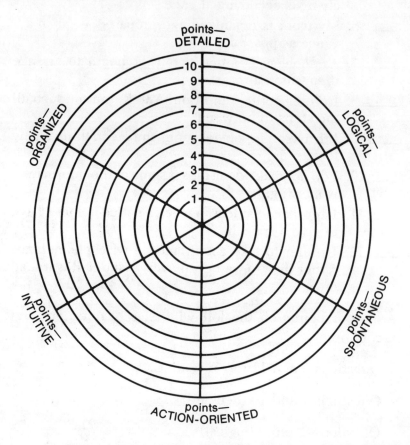

natural tendencies and the areas in which you need to improve. Note that these sketches illustrate the way you *prefer* to work, not necessarily the way you work under pressure.

Organized

Your strengths are in preparation. When a speech or briefing is set, you find out what is required, gather information, and prepare an outline, then a draft, and then a final copy. Several practices on tape or in front of a mirror add to your comfort. The drawback here is that you are so dependent on extensive preparation that question-and-answer sessions or late-breaking industry news can undermine your confidence because you cannot plan fully for them.

Detailed

Your strengths are in research. You investigate the topic thoroughly and gather every piece of relevant information. Then you construct your presentation to allow the audience to consider most of the items that led you to your conclusion.

You are respected for your thoroughness and your in-depth analysis. Your weakness is that you may bore listeners with such thoroughness. They wish you would glean the most critical elements, present them with a recommendation or conclusion, and sit down.

Logical

You know how to offer a clear, systematic exploration of your ideas. You approach issues by considering each relevant element and its relationship to the whole. You are good at identifying problem areas and applying rational, proven approaches to solving such problems. People respect your objectivity and your clarity of analysis. The problem with this style is that you sometimes fail to engage the attention and emotions of the audience—the very responses you need in order to move them to action. You may sound dry, sometimes boring.

Spontaneous

You have a natural ease with different people and in diverse situations. Although you may be shy about speaking, you warm up once you start. You are good at including the very latest news and information in your presentation because you are always aware of the world around you. People respect the nimbleness of your mind and thoughts. Sometimes, though, you trust your extemporaneous skill too much. You may fail to plan and prepare some parts of your presentation—especially the powerful opening and persuasive closing.

Action-Oriented

Your strengths are in focus and leadership. You recognize the need to act on information and to make decisions—sometimes without the luxury of complete information. You are willing to organize and assign work so that the project gets started. You help others focus their energy on getting results. People respect you for your vigor and assertiveness, but you have a tendency to be impatient. You may act too soon and push others into motion before the action is fully justified by the facts.

Intuitive

You operate successfully on the basis of your hunches. You synthesize information from many different sources and develop a feeling about which way to go. As the feeling becomes more concrete, you develop a vision of a desirable future outcome, and you know how to communicate that vision to others and enlist their support. Unfortunately, others who have not understood the vision clearly see you as a dreamer.

These, then, are the characteristics of your style. Notice that each characteristic has both strengths and snags. Note your two strongest and your two weakest characteristics. Ask yourself whether you would benefit from investing some time in developing all six areas. Here is one activity for each characteristic that could help you develop that quality.

Exercise: Organized

To become more organized, prepare for your next presentation, using the planning suggestions in Chapter 5. Commit yourself to twice the planning and practice you usually invest.

Exercise: Detailed

To become more detailed, gather twice as much information as usual for your next presentation. Review the data carefully. Consider whether there are additional sources you might draw upon. Locate all the information you can, even if you do not present it all.

Exercise: Logical

To become more logical, analyze the main topic of your next presentation more fully. Write the topic at the head of a blank page; then list causes, results, costs, benefits, or any other related factors. Arrange your information in a clear, orderly progression.

Exercise: Spontaneous

To become more spontaneous, ask a colleague to write 10 topics on slips of paper. Draw one slip a day, and instantly create and tape an unrehearsed 2- to 3-minute speech on that topic. Listen to the tapes, and notice how practice helps you improve. Welcome questions at the end of your next presentation, and apply your newfound nimbleness in answering them.

Exercise: Action-Oriented

To become more action-oriented, cut your next presentation content by one-third, and spend the extra time generating action on your topic. Use physical activity to help your mind get used to a shorter response time. Play computer games or racketball for an hour a week. Choose other activities that do not allow you the time you usually need for processing information. Help yourself become more comfortable moving from information to action.

Exercise: Intuitive

To become more intuitive, give yourself half a day to peruse three to five newspapers, books, or magazines. Read whatever appeals to you. After reading, relax. Take a walk, a swim, or a nap, idly asking yourself to come up with some common threads, themes, or patterns in what you read. Let the pattern emerge naturally until you sense a parallel to something in your industry. Use this insight in your next presentation.

The most significant thing about the Style Characteristics Profile is that it helps you to identify your natural style so you can work from there. You may blend or bend your style, but it is relatively permanent. If you are strongest in the top half of the circle, usually you will be good at preparing speeches. You may have to work on delivery skills. If you are strongest in the bottom characteristics, you will usually be good at delivering speeches. You may have to work on preparation skills.

You and Risk

What is your personal response to risk? We are not talking about whitewater rafting or roller coasters. We are talking about risks that can help you reach your goals. If you heard today about a toll-free number to a worldwide television network that you could call to express your views on some timely topic, would you call?

Small risk exercises help prepare you to be comfortable when larger challenges arise. If you are a person who avoids risk, you have little chance to make the mistakes later called "experience." Get out of those habits that are familiar and comfortable and embrace risks as learning opportunities. Why not volunteer to present a speech in the near future to a business, professional, or community group that is twice the size of the groups you usually address? If you do not ordinarily use a microphone, ask for one. Volunteer to go on local television in the 1-minute viewer speak-out on evening news. Keep your risk-taking self healthy, and it will be there when you need it.

Changing Style

Before tackling a change in style, you should recognize that you have been developing your style over many years, so change will not be instantaneous. But if you can keep the desired result firmly in mind, the benefits may be worth the effort.

Take your voice, for example. This is an area in which many people experience insecurity. "Is it too weak?" "Too low?" "Too high?" "Too shallow?" "Too soft?" From your first moments on earth, you have been practicing to speak the way you do. Your voice is deeply ingrained. But you *can* change it.

First, remember that you *learned* your voice, mostly from your family. People used to tell you, "You sound just like your brother (or your mother) on the phone." Each of us has the same physical apparatus for speaking. The influences of family, native language, and cultural environment all help shape how we use that apparatus. The nasal French sounds, the guttural German sounds, and the tonal Thai sounds are all possible on our current equipment. We just have not trained ourselves to use our full range. The good news about the fact that the voice is learned is that you can relearn it differently.

Just to put the challenge into perspective, figure out how many days you have been "practicing" your voice the way it is. At age 30 you have been practicing for 10,957 days; at age 40, for 14,603 days; age 50, for 18,256 days. If you could improve your voice in only a year, it would not be such a monumental task. Right? Here are the steps toward making a change.

1. Your initial response to recognizing something in your style that fails to get you the results you want, something that gets in your way, something that sabotages your efforts, is disgust. You simply do not like what you hear. The intensity of this dislike tells you that you are ready to invest significant energy in changing.

2. You begin to look for a stylistic alternative, something you like better, a model or a series of models that you can

work toward. You say to yourself, "I like what I see and hear. This person has a quality that could blend with my natural style to help produce the results I want." Developing a clear vision of your more desirable future state helps you maintain your resolve for long-term productive changes. Be as concrete and specific as possible in defining the outcome for yourself. What you can see clearly, you can be. If you care enough to define exactly what you want, you are much closer to creating it.

3. After defining the improvement you want to make, you say to yourself, "How will I be able to remember this once I look out at that audience?"

One powerful method to help you improve your voice is to use a "visual chime." The visual chime is a preselected object in your speaking room that triggers a pleasant "ding" in your head every time you catch a glimpse of it. That "sound" reminds you to use the new tone, pitch, or intensity—to practice your preferred behavior. In case you forget, why not take small blank pieces of paper and stick them on the wall at two or three places where your eyes wander naturally? Each time you see one, your visual chime will ring and you will remember to practice your change. No one else will even be aware of your on-the-platform training technique.

This technique also works for reminding you to smile more often, adapt your voice and gesture, maintain longer eye contact, or make whatever style change you wish.

4. Eventually, your new skill becomes automatic. The skill is now a part of your natural style. You say to yourself, "That was easy!" It is now time to pat yourself on the back and rest a moment before you select a new skill to work on.

Future Truth: An Allied Strategy

Your transition into the new skill will be much easier if you can begin to see and think of yourself as already operating at the new level. The language that we use to describe ourselves shapes our actions and reinforces the old way of doing things. Learn to describe yourself and your skills more optimistically, and you will grow into this "future truth" more easily. Just saying the words does not create change. It does, however, reinforce your promise to yourself and release you from the tyranny of old patterns. Here's a multipurpose formula: Formerly I . . . , and now I . . . . Here are a few examples:

- *Formerly* I was very nervous speaking to groups of 1000 or more, *and now* I am feeling more comfortable and confident in these situations.
- *Formerly* I was afraid people would ask me questions that I could not answer, *and now* I realize that I can admit when I do not have the information and arrange to get back to the audience.
- *Formerly* I spoke very woodenly and stiffly, *and now* I am using tonal variety and gestures more naturally.
- *Formerly* I was known for being technical and boring, *and now* I am incorporating examples and occasional humor into my presentations.
- *Formerly* my voice would become high and shrill, *and now* I am developing a deeper, richer tone.

In the hours and hours you spend each week talking to yourself about yourself, try changing what you say. It helps loosen you up for making changes. Stop saying, "I could never do that." Be sure to focus on only one or two closely linked items at a time. Improve that single area, and then pick a new one to tackle. This keeps you from scattering your focus and energy. Be patient in this campaign. The results are worth it!

One final note in working on improving your voice: Be

sure you really need to do this. Listen to yourself on audiotape for 2 or 3 hours before you decide to make changes. Ordinarily, you never hear your voice as others do. You usually hear yourself from inside your head, not outside through your ears. Therefore your voice sounds strange, unfamiliar, sometimes jarring on tape. Remember that different does not necessarily mean bad.

Ask the opinion of others you respect. You may get some surprising reassurance or some helpful, analytical feedback about whether your voice needs changing, and if so, what qualities to work on.

Toppling Presentation Barriers

Aristotle defined happiness as "the exercise of your vital abilities along lines of excellence in a life that affords them scope." Public speaking is one of life's vital abilities that can afford your life greater scope and happiness. But why is it so tough? There must be some basic fear here, some basic vulnerability.

Remember fifth grade? You survived writing the composition on "How I Spent My Summer Vacation," you survived the arithmetic review, and then you heard the dreaded sentence. "This semester we are going to work on speeches." Your assigned topic was "The Louisiana Purchase." Your friends got "Crops of Ancient Egypt" and "Printing in Colonial Days."

Why did we dread these talks so much? Why did they leave scars that persist even today? That is easy. These were subjects that you knew nothing about and your audience cared nothing about. You had no personal experience in the topic. You had no passion to draw on. You were afraid you would never be able to fill up the required 5 minutes. You were afraid you would freeze, and most

afraid that the other kids would actually ask questions at
the end. Remember the "Whew!" feeling of intense relief
when you sat down after such a speech? It was as if you
had escaped with your life, or at least your dignity.

But times have changed—now, you *do* know your subject. You have spent years living and learning your topic.
Your biggest challenge is to select from a wealth of information only those bits appropriate to your goal. Recognize
that even in a question-and-answer session you would usually know the answer, know of a resource where the answer could be found, or promise the questioner a later
response. Relax! You know what you are talking about. You
are no longer in the fifth grade!

Another problem underlying this phobia is the urge to
get it all out. You know you are suffering from this ailment
when you start to plan a presentation by asking yourself,
"How can I give them everything I have learned, thought,
read, and researched in the last 3 years in only 20 minutes?" The answer is that you cannot. There is no reason
you would want to. They certainly prefer that you do not
try!

Overcome this barrier by focusing instead on the one
significant thing you want to convey to that audience. Remember, your speech is not what comes out of your mouth.
It is what goes into your audience's heads, onto their "to
do" lists, and into next year's budget or contract.

A third barrier to speaking well comes from a puritanical
reverence for discipline. Many people sincerely feel that it
is somehow not dignified or professional to vary from a
formal, businesslike presentation of the facts. Speakers under this delusion prefer to stand behind the lectern and
read a dry text in an entirely bland, rational, controlled
style. They seek the predictable anonymity of "delivering
the paper" without looking the audience in the eyes. They
prefer safety to impact. They sacrifice the option to offer
both information and direction to the audience. If the audi-

ence finds it hard to listen to or remember what is said, they sniff defensively that the audience lacks discipline.

Ask yourself if your commitment to being professional, dignified, and formal is perhaps an excuse for staying with a presenting style you saw in school, one you have seen at professional meetings, one you have seen in the legislature. Remember, people speaking in such forums are more involved in being listed in the programs and getting into the record than in making a difference to today's sophisticated and media-wise audiences.

So remember, you should be *helping* your listeners, not criticizing them. Help them by engaging their eyes and their minds in exploring your proposal, your ideas, your product, your research. If presidents and popes use humor, examples, and illustrations to shape their messages more memorably for listeners, should you not do the same?

Key Ideas

- Your natural best speaking style is based on the kind of person you are.
- Your style blends six characteristics in varying proportions and intensities.
- Each blend has strengths and snags. Instead of trying to make dramatic changes, learn to capitalize on your strengths.
- Practice limited-risk exercises to explore beyond your comfort zone.
- Take charge of your voice or other specific areas you want to change.
- Identify and break through your barriers.

CHAPTER FOUR

All about Your Audience

Twelve Basic Truths

Who is your audience—3 decision makers in a board room, 30 colleagues in a planning meeting, or 300 conference participants? Whatever the specific makeup of that particular group, there are 12 basic truths about audiences.

The Audience Cocreates the Speech

They are your partners in whatever happens in that room. When you are in an audience and the speaker addresses you with assurance and skill, you assume a receptive mental attitude to allow the speaker's thoughts into your awareness. When someone speaks with a faltering, hesitant, mumbling style, your mind begins to buzz with questions. "What's wrong with this person or these ideas that he cannot present them more confidently?" "Do I have to sit here and listen to another 30 minutes of this stuff?" The presenter's ease in speaking puts the audience at ease in listening. The speaker's nervousness, inexperience, or modesty awakens audience concerns about the speaker's credibility and the integrity of her or his proposals or ideas. You owe your audience "partners," your cocreators, a skilled delivery so that they can concentrate on your major message.

The Audience Wants You to Win

They are spending an irretrievable part of their lives listening to you. They want you to do well. If you do not succeed, they, too, are disappointed—something few of us enjoy. Ninety-eight percent of your audience is truly hoping for your success. Whether your purpose is to inform, to persuade, to teach, to inspire, or to entertain them, if you do not succeed, they will have wasted their time. But, of course, there is always truth number three.

Two Percent Are There to See You Fail

These are the people who attend races with telephoto lens cameras loaded with high-speed color film, sit on "Dead Driver's Curve," and hope for the best—a spectacular pileup. They thrive on disasters—other people's disasters.

These people derive a perverse sense of security from any inkling of ineffectiveness you display. Their image of themselves rises as their awe of you comes down a notch. They think life is graded, "on the curve." These predators are there no matter what your topic or tone. Whether you are scholarly or informal, deliberate or humorous, anecdotal or statistical, 2 percent of the audience will celebrate your inadequacies.

Their level of criticism is enormously subtle. You need not mispronounce words, have a slide upside down in the projector, or quote a questionable statistic as if it were truth. The connoisseur of criticism will notice that your suit clashes with the backdrop, that your use of pauses makes some of the audience restless, that you are putting on weight, or that your hair is thin on top.

Here is the reassuring thought to remember. You do not need to plan to satisfy these people. They will achieve their goal no matter what you do. And they, too, will be pleased afterward. What more could you ask for? Above all, avoid trying to win them over. They are here on their own mission, and they will succeed. Using your energies to convert these crusaders cheats you and the rest of the audience. Focus on the 98 percent, and let the 2 percent take care of themselves.

The Audience Expects Polish

Our expectations have escalated. We have seen professional speakers, educators, politicians, religious and community leaders, executives, and sports personalities speak before us and on television. We are impatient with the old "unaccustomed as I am to public speaking" approach. We expect our leaders and executives to *be* accustomed. Your audience expects you to handle ideas and language skillfully. They expect you to be graceful and gracious with an occasional touch of humor or lightness. They expect you to avoid sexist or racist language and any comments in seriously questionable taste. They expect you to handle most timely and related questions on the spot or to know when and how answers can be obtained. They expect you to handle hostile challenges well without taking it out on them.

Audience Members Have Different Styles of Thinking and Listening

Recent investigations of how the brain works reveal this: Each person's brain has areas of specialization and preference. Just as we describe ourselves as being right-handed or left-handed, even though we use both hands comfortably most of the time, so also do we tend to be predominantly "right-brained" or "left-brained."

Of course, the whole brain is operating all the time. It is just that we tend to be lazy. We tend to prefer information which is packaged to appeal to "home plate" for our brain. We prefer the language, examples, and approach of "home." Here is a brief summary of the four styles of listening you can expect in any audience. The *mover* and *arranger* are left-brain styles. The *visionary* and *relater* are right-brain styles.

- The *mover* is quick-thinking and action-oriented. Critics see the mover as a bully because of strong leadership or take-charge tendencies. Movers listen best to brief, logical summaries with recommended solutions. They may veto the solution and substitute one of their own, but the focus stays on speed and action.
- The *arranger* is oriented toward thoroughness and detail. Critics see the arranger as a plodder because of the time and attention he or she invests. Arrangers listen best to detailed, accurate, thorough, and sequential presentations. They read any supplementary material you provide. They can be difficult to sway to your view, but once convinced, they stand loyal and firm.
- The *visionary* is oriented toward the global view. Critics see the visionary as a dreamer because she or he looks beyond things as they are now to things as they might be. Visionaries listen best to goals and purpose first. Then they will accept elements that go into creating desired results.
- The *relater* values people and relationships. Critics see the relater as a cheerleader or social director because of the enthusiastic "people" focus. Relaters listen best to human impact information. How will people feel about this? What will they do?

Again, remember that all people exhibit all four styles in different intensities and proportions. Notice, therefore, how the outlines and examples in Chapter 5 accommodate all four styles.

Are there any handy tips for assessing the likely style of an audience you are preparing to address? If you are working with a group made up entirely of people from one profession or field, determine which quadrant best describes the average member of that group and pitch your talk in those terms. Engineers and accountants, for example, are often *arrangers*, while sales people are often *relaters*. Usually, though, it is safer to assume your audience will contain all types of thinkers. So plan to reach as many as possible as often as possible.

Chapter 3 emphasized that you start from the strengths of your natural style. Your instinct will be to plan the entire presentation in the style which matches yours. "That is the best, most normal, most natural way to think," you believe. Beware. This chauvinistic attitude can cost you votes, approvals, raises, contracts, and clients. Respect people's thinking differences. They add great variety to life. Start from your natural style, and ask yourself what else you need to add to accommodate all styles with logic, visual, emotional, and action-oriented material.

In business presentations we usually expect an emphasis on logic, reason, and knowledge. You may appropriately concentrate on these areas. But do not ignore the other bases, or you will lose much of your impact.

The Audience's Natural State is Boredom

We are victims of the "million-dollar minute" mentality in this country. To broadcast a commercial during the Superbowl football game has cost over $1 million per minute since 1985. And that is just air time. It does not include creating the commercial. Think of the pressure this places on advertisers. No wonder they constantly bombard us with shorter message units. Whether you watch much television or not, our culture is being educated to absorb, understand, and finally *prefer* shorter messages.

So as you look out across the boardroom or the convention hall before you step to the podium, you will see some people yawning and others looking at their watches. Here you are, full of adrenaline and ready to go; they are yawning. So assume they will start out bored.

Plan your presentation for the greatest impact in the least time possible. Be as dynamic and dramatic as your dignity and role allow—and stretch that occasionally to extend your range. Remember you are constantly battling their powerful natural state of boredom. Help them listen!

They Listen Visually More than Verbally

Communication analyst Albert Mehrabian did some interesting research on the effectiveness of communication channels. According to Mehrabian, we take meaning from the messages we receive in the following proportions: 7 percent from the words themselves—the dictionary meaning of the vocabulary we hear; 38 percent from voice and vocal qualities, including rate, pitch, tone, volume, and intensity; 55 percent from nonverbal cues—posture, stride, gestures, eye contact, facial expressions, mannerisms, and movement.

Test this yourself. Stand in front of a mirror and say naturally, "I am depressed." Now say the same words in a hearty voice with your hands raised triumphantly in the air over your head. Which is the strongest signal in the second version? Observers say the strongest message is the nonverbal one of triumph. Now put this information to work. Attend to the visual elements of your message. And bear in mind three essential facts:

- When you use visual aids, slides, or overhead illustrations, you make your message more memorable.
- When you use actual props, models, or concrete objects, the message becomes even stronger.
- *You* are always your most vital visual aid. Use your eyes, your facial expressions, your gestures, your posture, and your stride to communicate the tone of your message. Use the pictures you can create with your

words and your voice to flesh out your ideas—to give them shape and form in the mind of your listeners.

By carefully crafting all three aspects—words, vocal, and visual—you will ensure greater impact.

Audiences Respond Best to Specifics—Facts, Humor, Examples, Stories, Involvement

Put your message on a concrete level as often as possible. (This sentence is not yet verbally concrete.) Tell the audience about a specific day, time, and event that helped make the particular idea clear to you. (This sentence is more concrete.) Say to the audience, "Last Tuesday as I drove 6 miles to work in the morning rain, I heard a news item on the radio that you need to remember as you vote today. It seems this retired couple had put their savings . . . ." (These sentences are even more concrete.)

The longer you talk about abstractions (peace, prosperity, productivity, motivation, etc.), the harder it is to maintain quality control over what the listeners are thinking. Here is an experiment to demonstrate that idea. Stop and ask 10 colleagues to tell you the first thing that pops into their minds when you say a word. Use an abstract term such as *productivity, motivation,* or *the good life.* Then try a concrete term or phrase on them, for instance, *the green coat* or *a mature skier brimming with vitality.* Record their responses for you to review when planning your next presentation.

When you use abstract language, people are usually very busy making the abstract concrete in their own minds according to their own definitions. Even as they listen, they are constantly creating their own versions of what they are hearing. Their unconscious question is, What does this mean to me?

When you use concrete language, you help shape the audience's personal version of your speech to keep it closer to *your* version. They listen differently and better because you have changed their unconscious question to What next? instead of What's that?

If you are speaking in technical or business subjects, you often object, "But that takes too long. I will never cover all the information." You have been trained to think that your audiences are too sophisticated to need such pampering. Do not assume anything too quickly; experiment in some low-risk settings so you will be ready when the stakes are high.

The proportions of successful speeches may vary from 95 percent technical, 5 percent illustrative to 50 percent technical, 50 percent illustrative to 5 percent technical, 95 percent illustrative. Find out which works best for you and when. You may be surprised to learn that highly knowledgeable audiences respond very well to the last combination in the appropriate circumstances.

Audiences Have Physical, Mental, and Chemical Distractions

Here are some stark realities. People become hungry and thirsty at frequent intervals. They need to stand, to stretch, to move, to go to the bathroom. Some need coffee or cigarettes. Some need to call the office to check on today's crisis. Some need a few moments of silence in an empty staircase.

How does this fact affect you, the speaker? If their bodies are speaking to them more loudly and more urgently than your words, to whom do you think they will listen?

You have a commitment to them and to yourself to deliver your information as well as possible. If you realize, however, that they are past the point of productive listening, why continue? Remember that they are your partners in creating this speech. And it is a game where everybody wins or nobody does. You cannot give a great speech to a restless audience.

Learn from a renowned educator who was guest speaker at a large university's graduation. The event started nearly on time but dragged 5 or 10 minutes over schedule on each segment. The diplomas were awarded, and the guest speaker was introduced 45 minutes after the commencement was scheduled to end. The speaker was introduced; approached the lectern; looked out over 2000 faces full of pride, pleasure, satisfaction, restlessness, and respectful patience, and began; "All my life I have wished for a standing ovation. If you will give me one, I will sit down." A few seconds of astonished silence were broken by an unprecedented cheering ovation. At that time, by that speaker, for that audience, in that situation, it was the best possible speech. Do you remember the key point of the speech at your graduation? These alumni will never forget theirs!

If this extreme alternative is too radical for you, what other choices do you have? You might select one of these options or preferably blend all four:

1. Recognize and admit the audience's discomfort. "Our program chair and I recognize that my next 25-minute segment is going to run us over schedule and may cut into previous arrangements you have made." *Rationale:* This keeps the audience from fidgeting, looking at their watches, and saying to themselves, "Does the speaker not know what time it is?"

2. Negotiate a listening contract. "I can cut my presentation to 15 minutes with no session time for questions. I will need you to help by listening extra carefully because I will be covering some of the material rapidly." *Rationale:* Although people tend not to use their focused listening skills often, they are capable of consciously choosing to listen carefully, especially when asked to.

3. Legitimize leaving. "For those who must leave on

schedule, the results will be reported in the Journal next spring. I am sorry you cannot stay." *Rationale:* Some people really must leave. This statement lets the rest of the group know you will not be distracted or upset by these few, so they need not be distracted either.

4. Have a brief stretch break. "Let us take a stretch break for a few seconds just to relax and refocus. Anyone who must leave can move toward the back. Ready, stretch." *Rationale:* This helps the audience focus for better listening, it breaks their sitting tension, and it allows some crowd movement without much distraction.

If your presentation is too essential to condense, consider negotiating with the planner to cut program time elsewhere, to put you on somewhere else in the schedule, or to mail out the full text of your presentation to all attendees.

Your Audience is Less Involved in Your Topic than You Are

You came to give this speech because you are informed about and involved in the topic. Some of your audience may have come for similar reasons. Others came in just to rest their feet or because they had to. It is safe to assume that their usual reaction before you talk about your specific idea or proposal is indifference. It is safest to attempt to move them only slightly, but positively, in your direction. Rather than try to convert them, why not set a goal to move them from indifference to intrigue? Move them to a state in which they are receptive to, perhaps eager for, more information on the issue.

If you are there to promote a specific product, do not insist that they buy at this point; just ask them to agree to come to a demonstration next week. If you are presenting a policy proposal, do not insist on having it passed. Accept the audience's offer to review the documentation and discuss it at the next session. Give them some avenues to follow to satisfy that initial tickle of interest. Where will they go for more information? What areas of world or national news should they be tracking to stay current? What authorities should they trust or challenge? When is the next big breakthrough expected in this area?

Know the limitations, and thus the possibilities, of your forum. Set your sights on what can be accomplished. Then aim a notch or two higher.

They Respond More to Less

One to three key ideas with supporting examples are plenty for a 30-minute presentation. Avoid the temptation to spill "27 Key Secrets to Professional Success" in one presentation. The audience will be more likely to listen, remember, and act on your information if you keep your presentation brief, yet vivid and detailed.

Research tells us that people tend to remember up to seven items in a series. Additional items turn to mush in our heads. Do not push the audience that hard. Stop speaking before they stop listening.

They Need to Know What to Do Next

Unless they are listening purely for entertainment, your audience needs to know what to *do* as a result of listening. What action do you want them to take? This central idea governs everything you say and do. Do not expect the audience to figure it out for themselves. Close your presentation with specific instructions for an action they should take. Tell them to pass your budget, elect your candidate, give you the job, donate to the cause, write to their senator, or consider the new design.

Tell them what to do, and, if possible, link that recommendation to something they are likely to do in the next 24 hours. This helps create in them a "timed-release" reminder of their intention to act. Use phrases such as "Tomorrow morning when you face yourself in the mirror as you brush your teeth, say to yourself, 'This is the day I . . .' " or "The next time you set foot in an automobile, ask yourself if you should . . . " or "Tonight when you take off your shoes and your feet revel in having their delicious freedom back, say to yourself . . . ."

Your Specific Audience

Given that the 12 characteristics describe audiences in general, let us look at your specific audience. It is helpful to ask the meeting planner many questions. You may want to use the following Audience Profile Questionnaire to gather information and avoid future blushing. (Yes, I once honestly said to a meeting coordinator, "Tell me about your people, broken down by age and sex." The reply? "Age has gotten to a few, but sex does not seem to be hurting any of them.") Even if you yourself are a primary force behind the planning of the meeting, you will want to analyze the audience with regard to these 12 characteristics.

Audience Profile Questionnaire

1. Name of organization:
2. Type of event:
3. Length of presentation:
4. Intent of presentation (inform, persuade, teach, inspire, entertain):
5. Number of people expected:

6. Job categories:

7. Job locations:

8. Approximate salary range:

9. Educational background:

10. Topic/title:

11. Theme of event:

12. Action goal:

13. Audience mood:

14. Audience interest in topic:

15. Background and knowledge in topic:

16. Issues and concerns that most affect the audience:

17. Possible areas of challenge or resistance:

18. Social chatter topics: What will they be talking about among themselves at the reception?

19. Additional comments:

Not being prepared can lead to embarrassing mistakes. A colleague of mine once gave a speech in which he made the remark, "So if you are making just $100,000 a year for the next 10 years, you are talking about $1 million." This particular audience had salaries averaging far below that figure. Several of the audience later admitted to being distracted by the disparity between that example and reality. Others thought the speaker insensitive for implying that their salaries were low. An irreverent few wondered what the speaker was earning for this speech.

Disparity in the opposite direction is also distracting. Therefore, why not ask the meeting planner these simple questions to help tailor your presentations more appropriately? Let us take a closer look at each item on the questionnaire.

•*Name of Organization.* This may seem like an obvious question, but in this age of "alphabet soup" company names, you are wise to check the exact name of the company, the organization, and the unit you are addressing. A recent speaker at IBM confused the members of the Federal Systems Division by calling them the Federal Services Division—a small mistake, but one that rang in the ears of the audience.

Type of Event. Is this a board retreat, a sales meeting, a manager's conference, a training session, an educational seminar, a convention session, or a gathering of the world congress? The type of event will give you important clues about the audience.

Length of Presentation. This tells you what the planned time contract is for accomplishing your objectives. Ask the planner how firm this figure is. Does the group have a record of arriving late? Do morning programs usually run late, cutting into the afternoon schedule? Is this the last spot on a panel of babblers? In an ideal preparation, you can exactly match the planned time slot or even cut up to 25 percent of the time without sacrificing any of your objectives.

Intent of Presentation. Are you there primarily to inform, persuade, teach, inspire, or entertain? Focus on your intent to recognize how best to reach this audience.

Number of People Expected. There are six categories of audience size:

Private = 1 person

Board = 2 to 12 people

Class = 13 to 35 people

Small Group = 36 to 150 people

Medium Group = 150 to 500 people

Large Group = 500 plus

Most professionals say they are comfortable in two or three of the categories, but that the other categories make them nervous. Not surprisingly, some people who are comfortable in groups of 2000 feel awkward in one-on-one situations. Often people who are good one on one do not like to talk to groups of more than 50 people.

Group size influences many of your choices, such as when to use a microphone, visual aids, or handouts. Size has the greatest influence, though, on your mental preparation.

Do not let large groups intimidate you. Remember, once swayed positively in your direction, large groups provide an enormous positive force toward generating the impact you want.

•*Job Category.* Who are these people? What are their titles? Do you have a fairly homogeneous group, or are there people from all parts of the organization?

•*Job Locations.* How many live locally and will be commuting to the meeting? How many will be staying there? Have people come from Alaska and Ireland? What will make their trip worthwhile?

•*Approximate Salary Range.* What is the range of salaries of people who are attending? What recreation and sports do they enjoy? Are health and fitness popular topics? To what extent is money a motivator for these people? Do they earn commissions or bonuses?

•*Educational Background.* What kind of degrees or educational background do they have? What newspapers and magazines do they read? What types of books do they talk about? How intellectual or technically oriented might they be?

•*Topic/Title.* What is the specific topic and focus of your presentation?

•*Theme.* Is there an overall conference or meeting theme? How does your topic tie in with that theme?

•*Action Goal.* What is it you want them to do as a result of hearing your speech?

•*Audience Mood.* How will they be thinking and feeling when they walk into the room? Are they likely to be bright

and expectant or lazy and tired? Are they coming off ban-
ner success or recovering from a slump?

•Interest in Topic. How much do they care about this
topic? What is in it for them?

•Background in and Knowledge of Topic. How much do
they already know? How much will you have to define;
how much can you take for granted?

•Issues and Concerns that Affect Them. What elements of
your message will affect the audience most directly? Are
there any important indirect elements?

•Possible Areas of Resistance. What are the likely areas of
resistance, and how intense will that resistance be? How
can that resistance be rechanneled into constructive energy?

•Social Chatter Topics. Dr. Richard Berendzen, President
of American University, asks meeting planners this question to get at the heart of what is going on in the lives of
audience members: "What do they talk about over cock-
tails at the reception? Is it cash flow, mortgages, kids in
college, employees, the government, food?" The answer to
this question helps him have a closer feel for the pulse of
the group.

•Additional Comments. Any other special issues that
emerge—any big product unveilings, sales contests, pleasant office gossip, retirements, etc., you might refer to?

"But is it not a lot of work to do all this?" you ask. Sure.
And it is as legitimate a part of your presentation as preparing your outline, remarks, handouts, and visual aids. The
better you understand the audience, the better the job you
will do for them—and for yourself. Make the commitment.
If 500 people listen to you for 30 minutes, that is 250 hours
of professional time you are responsible for. If their time is
worth $10 an hour, that comes to $2500; at $25 an hour,
$6250; at $50 an hour, $12,500; and at $100 an hour,
$25,000. With that responsibility on your shoulders, is it

not wise to invest another few hours to find out more about the group?

Using the questionnaire helps in two powerful ways. First, it helps you focus on the needs and interests of the audience, your cocreators. This gives you much greater ease and assurance that you are going in front of people you "know." You are better prepared, more relaxed, and comfortable. Second, it helps you select the language and examples that bring the messages home to the audience. They follow your ideas well because they feel that you have taken the time to understand your audience.

How to Change for Different Audiences

"I have seen my boss speak one way in a proposal session, another way at the convention, and a third way in an employee training session. He is successful in all three settings. Is that just instinct, or can I plan those adaptations in my presentations?"

There are five stances from which to speak. Each has a distinctive base of power and a distinctive approach.

1. *Boss.* This stance is based on authority. You are in the decision-making role. You may welcome input, but you retain the right to make the decision. When speaking from the *boss* stance, you may want to draw on your organization's mission, policies, goals, and procedures for support.

2. *Expert.* This stance is based on knowledge and experience. You are the acknowledged leader in your specialty. You share information and correct misinformation. You draw on your background, experience, and research; and

you stay current in all the latest developments in your area.

3. *Colleague*. This stance is based on equality. You seek to present and share information while being wholly open to discovering new information from others. You draw on your expanding understanding in an area you are exploring.

4. *Sister/Brother*. This stance is based on concern and warmth. You appeal to the family spirit of a healthy working team to try to inform, persuade, or inspire listeners. This is often an effective stance for coaching individuals or groups to better performance. It protects others from the possibly smothering qualities of parental leadership, keeps you more approachable than the boss or expert, and lets the audience know you have a caring investment in their success.

5. *Novice*. This stance is based on enthusiasm. You share recent discoveries and their meaning with the audience. While you admit to the lack of a comprehensive background, you are exceptionally informed about recent discoveries and have immersed yourself in this topic. The freshness of your approach and your vitality renew or awaken the interest of your audience.

Let us look at how all five roles are appropriate for owners of small businesses in presentations made in one quarter. Carol and Frank Orlando run a small business in the Midwest. At the start of their fiscal year, July 1, Frank holds a session for their 19 employees to provide an overview of the coming year. He speaks in the role of boss. On July 10 Carol speaks from the expert role to a client. Her company is proposing a blanket purchasing system for all the client's supplies in the coming year, and she has all the facts at her command. In August the two share the platform at the annual convention of their professional society on the topic "More than 2 Percent: Experiences at Getting a Better Return on Direct Mail." This presentation is done from the colleague stance. On September 1, Frank presents his session for outside salespeople on time and territory management. Experience has shown him that this subject has more influence when it is taught from the brotherly, rather than the boss, stance. At the end of September, Carol addresses the local chamber of commerce on the delights and disasters of trying to use videotape feedback in training sessions with employees. She freely admits to being an enthusiastic novice in this area.

Clarity about your correct stance helps you in preparation, in delivery, and especially in thinking about the question-and-answer period. Unless you are in the role of expert, you need not be the slightest bit embarrassed by not having the answer to a question and promising to get back to the audience. The colleague, brother/sister, or novice might indeed ask for an answer from others in the audience who might have that specific information. Knowing your stance keeps you in balance.

Orchestrating the Environment

Another area in which a small investment of time pays large dividends is attending to the environment of the presentation. The best preparation falls flat when you are confronted with a nonfunctioning microphone, arctic or tropical room temperature, or the revivalist fervor of a raucous group in the adjoining ballroom.

Professional speaker Danny Cox advises visiting the site of the meeting well beforehand to check on the following five essential items. Be sure you know who on the hotel staff or conference staff can assist in making necessary adjustments.

Sound

Can your voice be heard easily in all sections of the room? Are the microphone tone and volume set properly? It is better to have the volume set slightly louder than you might first assume. This allows you to speak in a natural, comfortable tone and to drop to a near whisper for emphasis. It also allows for the fact that a large crowd "soaks up" some of the sound. Crowd members also make distracting coughs and other noises. Finally, it is good to remember that many people are hearing-impaired. High volume helps keep them with you throughout the presentation.

Air

Is there adequate ventilation? Have nonsmoking areas, based on air ventilation, been designated and marked? Should you ban smoking entirely? Are there blowers or other motors that will click on and interfere with your being heard by everyone? If windows or doors need to be open, can areas around them be kept clear and quiet?

Light

Is there appropriate light for the speaker, and for visual aids or props you plan to use? Lighting for the speaker is very poorly done in most meeting places, even some that pride themselves on being up-to-date conference and meeting facilities. Picture, for example, at the typical hotel ballroom or conference center the "flexible meeting space" area. If your session is in two or four sections of the flexible area, the lectern is usually positioned just in front of the folding panels, at the midpoint of the room. And no lights are trained there. The speaker stands in the dullest, grayest, most shadowed part of the room.

The solution? Request a spotlight. Assure yourself that people in the audience can see your face and can get the messages of your body language. Your visual information is an important element of dynamic delivery. Do not let lack of lighting cheat your audience. Do not stand in the gloom with only the reflected lectern light creating vampire shadows on your face.

Check lighting for the audience also. Do they have enough light to get safely into and out of their seats? Do they need light to take notes? Start to observe how lighting is used to influence moods. When the romantic singer comes on, the house lights dim. They come back up again for comedy. People respond instinctively to light.

Temperature

The empty meeting room should be uncomfortably cool, but not arctic. The bodies amassed there, each at 98.6 degrees Fahrenheit, will raise the room temperature quickly. The ideal room temperature is one at which most of the attendees are comfortable in the style of clothing appropriate to the occasion and season. Temperature is the first thing you check because it takes a long time for any adjustment to be felt.

Seating

If you are asked your preference for chair placement, consider requesting an angled row or a curved one. As people listen to you, their eyes naturally wander. Curved or angled rows allow them to browse over the faces of others. This browsing lets them watch how others react to your message and gives them more to think about. In straight rows people are usually looking only at the backs of heads. And there is not much of a message there.

Whatever the chair placement, take a tip from professional speaker, Joel Weldon, and rope off the back of the room. This can be done easily with ribbon, string, tape, or

SEATING ARRANGEMENTS

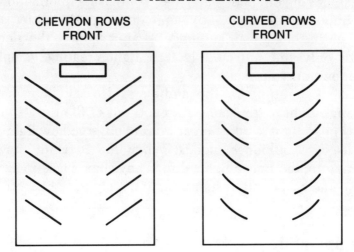

long strips. Roping off this section encourages people to sit up front and gets the group better distributed in the room. As the front seats fill, open up the back section farthest from the door. Save the area nearest the door for late-comers. Protect the on-time attendees from being stumbled over by latecomers.

Here is another element of room psychology: People prefer to sit near aisles, so avoid rows that touch the walls. Try for three to five usable aisles to increase audience comfort. People's resistance to you and your ideas increases if they feel trapped by where they are sitting.

Read Your Listeners as You Speak

In addition to the time and attention the audience deserves in your preparation, they deserve attention as you speak. Watch their faces, their fidgeting, their early departures.

Learn to dance with them—you lead, they follow. If you feel they are not quite in step with you, apply some kindly, guiding pressure as you would with a dance partner.

But how do you know when they are in step? How can you identify key messages that you are getting through to them? How can you turn your instinct that you are succeeding into an observable reality? As you notice each item listed below, remember that audience members are reacting to many factors, of which you are only one. Do not take their reactions too personally.

I learned this lesson from someone who left halfway through one of my speeches years ago. I had been concerned because her departure was so abrupt and visible and took place during a controversial part of my proposal. She returned after the session had ended, slightly breathless, to apologize. "I hated to leave," she said, "but I have a bid in on a house I want, and if I did not get through to the lawyer by 4 P.M., the house would have been gone. That is the only thing that would have dragged me away." Now if people leave my session early, I assume that real estate agents are thriving.

Another person taught me not to overreact to facial responses. Someone I worked closely with on a board of directors was attending one of my sessions. His frowns and grimaces concerned me deeply because we were usually in harmony on most issues. After the meeting I took him aside to ask what was wrong. His reply, "I had oral surgery this morning and my mouth is really hurting. By the way, you did a great job." Now if people frown, I assume that oral surgeons are thriving.

Still another person arrived 30 minutes late for a 60-minute session and had the effrontery to ask if I had a tape of the first part because he so hated to miss it. He had been detained getting a $128 traffic ticket for waiting on the roadside for the express lane to open at 9 A.M. "But it will be worth it," he said, "if I can copy your tape." You guessed it: Now when people come in late, I assume that law enforcement is thriving.

Do not take these apparent slights too personally. But *do* start to notice the following four clues that people are with you:

1. People vote with their feet, and they vote with their seat. The fact that people showed up, sat down, and stayed is one thing you can observe. The first reading you take on an audience is that they are there. Related item—always aim your efforts at the full chairs. Ignore the empty ones. As the opera singer commented, "I never sing to velvet." Although it is disappointing to prepare for 500 and get 15, do not let that feeling get in the way of doing the best job possible for those who came.

2. People smile, nod, look puzzled, take notes, and otherwise acknowledge that they hear you. Smiles and nods usually indicate agreement (or pleasant unrelated fantasies). Keep that calculator behind your eyes clicking. Notice the overall audience tapestry of smiles and frowns as you are introduced, and watch for changes as you speak. If a great many people look puzzled, simplify your explanation.

3. People respond to your questions. If you ask for a show of hands on an issue, they respond. "How many are using the KC 1904 system?" A majority of the group respond.

4. People ask questions. They ask insightful and challenging questions when you offer them the opportunity.

The job of reading the audience takes attention. This is why the scripted text is so difficult to deliver effectively— you have to read the text and the audience at once.

How to Avoid Offending an Audience with Sexist Language

Congratulations on being aware of the importance of this issue. Both women and men are diminished by language which discounts the contribution of half the population. More importantly, use of sexist language can interfere with getting your message across. No, you do not have to use the clumsy *he and she, hers and his,* or other awkward forms of gender balancing. Just develop an alertness to your use of language and examples. Here are five techniques you can practice over time to ensure gender-balanced language:

1. Avoid male and female stereotypes. Lawyers, doctors, senators, astronauts, secretaries, nurses, and executives come in both genders. Therefore, do not refer to a "lady senator" or a "male nurse."

2. Alternate female and male examples in your stories and illustrations.

Before	*After*
Managers comment on their sales staff, saying, "He is all fired up and motivated" or "He is relentless in cold calls."	Managers comment on their sales staff, saying, "She is all fired up and motivated" or "He is relentless in cold calls."

3. Restructure your sentence.

Before	*After*
Select someone good as chairman of the committee.	Select someone good to chair the committee.

4. Shift to the plural.

Before

When a manager goes on a trip, he should save all his receipts.

After

When managers go on business trips, they should save all their receipts.

5. Find substitutes for nouns that contain the word *man* or *woman*. Consider these examples:

Manhours	Staff hours, work hours
Businessman	Executive, professional
Fireman	Firefighter
Policeman	Police officer
Salesmen	Clerks, sales representatives
Cleaning woman	Office cleaner
Manpower	Labor force, workforce
Insurance man	Insurance agent
Statesman	Leader, politician
Man's achievements	Human achievements

Do not become paranoid about your language. So far nobody seems seriously in favor of changing all language—*personhole cover* is not threatening the traditional *manhole cover*. Do, however, be aware of the overall gender tone of your speech, and make some effort to bring that tone into balance with today's equal-opportunity environment.

The other side of this issue is that you should avoid being distracted by the occasional sexist language you may hear in another person's presentation. Terms such as *the little lady* or *the girls at the office* can be used quite innocently by otherwise enlightened leaders. People born in a certain time or living today in a genteel environment may not recognize that such terms raise hackles. Remember

Eleanor Roosevelt's comment that no one could make her feel inferior without her own cooperation. Unless you feel that certain language is used intentionally to diminish the significance and contribution of women, men, minorities, or other specific groups, forget it and concentrate on key ideas.

What If They Have Been Drinking?

Looking out at listeners engaged in a food fight is frightening, but it sometimes happens. Check whether your presentation is scheduled after a social hour, wine and cheese fest, or reception. Any cocktail event of an hour or longer is likely to produce a few partying spirits. These partying spirits may be loud, sociable, and boisterous; or they may be asleep in the mashed potatoes. What they all have in common is a very short attention span.

The best way to handle this challenge is to be sure it never happens to you. If it does, though, keep it light and keep it short. The worst thing you can do is to try to stay with your 30-minute speech and keep saying "Shhhh" to the revelers. Sarcasm is also a poor choice: "We will get to business here if our rowdy juvenile delinquents will start acting their age." Brief comments tied to humor or emotion with perhaps one idea to support them have the best chance of getting through to the majority of the audience. Avoid slides, use of overhead projectors, or anything else which might make your remarks longer or more serious.

Two brief stories follow. A colleague was once faced with an audience of 30 tables of listeners after a banquet. One table near the front had celebrated heartily during dinner. Their laughter and nudging continued throughout the speaker's introduction. The speaker opened by saying that there was a surprise door prize. The people at one "mystery table" would be treated to a free round of drinks in the lounge immediately. Not surprisingly, the rowdy revelers' table won. They departed. The rest of the group breathed an audible sigh of relief—the distracting members had safely departed for the lounge and their hotel rooms upstairs. The appreciative audience gave full attention to the short and stimulating address.

On another occasion a respected national speaker was commissioned to do a 40-minute after-dinner talk. Seeing that many of the group seemed drunk, he asked the meeting planner to let him cut the talk to about 10 minutes. The planner refused. "We hired you for your full talk. We are paying you for your full talk. And you are going to deliver your full talk, so help me God." (The planner was a little drunk, too.) The speaker offered to forgo the fee. The planner was firm. The speaker began, spoke with great effort, and did not receive much attention for 7 minutes. Then he looked at his watch and remarked, "I see our 40 minutes are almost up. Here is a parting thought for you . . ." No one commented on the true length of the talk. The planner reassured the speaker, "See, son, I knew you could do it!"

Key Ideas

- The audience is your partner in creating this speech. Know and trust them.
- Understand the 12 basic truths about audiences in general.
- Research each specific audience by completing the Audience Profile Questionnaire.
- Learn how to change your presentation to suit different audiences.

- Structure your presentation and the environment to help the audience listen well.
- Observe and respond to audience feedback the whole time you are speaking.
- Avoid sexist language.
- Learn to handle an audience who have been drinking.

CHAPTER FIVE

The Substance Side of the Coin

The Iceberg Formula

Remember the two sides of the coin—style and substance? Substance is what you say in your speech—the content. In selecting what to say out of your extensive background and experience, focus on your desired outcome or result. Then apply the *iceberg formula*.

Think about the great speakers you have heard. One reason they made your list of greats is that they had broad-based knowledge in their specialties and they were clearly current on the newest developments. There was a power behind that knowledge, a hidden reservoir of much greater knowledge than met the eye. They were giving you the visible part of the iceberg and letting the mountain below stay invisible; yet the mountain of ice below the surface supported the tip you could see.

Such a speaker leaves most audiences hungering for more. A hungry audience will be moved to action. They are more inclined to explore further or seek results. A merely satisfied group, however, may walk away thinking, "That is nice. I wonder what is on the late show tonight."

The point of a presentation is not to satisfy the audience so much that they become complacent. It is to stimulate them into action or thought. If you fully understand what you want them to do as a result of listening, use this understanding to assess how much of the iceberg they need to see. Rarely will they need to know more than 15 percent of what you know to be so moved. Be careful not to continue giving them knowledge when what they need from you is inspiration to *act*.

Work Backward from the Bottom Line

The first question most of us ask when faced with a speaking opportunity is "What am I going to say?" It may be more productive to define the "bottom line" and work backward from that.

If the purpose of your presentation is to move the audience to action, that is the bottom line. Focus on what you want them to do as a result of listening, and prepare the ending of your speech first. Once you have decided on the ending, you can devise a powerful opening. Such an opening does three things. First, it gets attention. Second, it provides a bridge between whatever the members of the audience were thinking about before you started to speak and whatever you wish them to focus on now. Third, it previews the bottom-line closing.

Note that many successful presentations seem to have a circular structure—the end comes back to a reference, quote, or story from the beginning. This device provides a strong sense of completion and lets the audience know you prepared carefully out of respect for their time and attention.

Now that you have a rousing opening and a powerful closing, plan the body of your presentation. Limit yourself to two or three main ideas, and illustrate each with a variety of statistics, examples, illustrations, stories, songs, quotes, visual aids, magic tricks, props, or whatever else holds their attention and keeps them listening. Refer to the

Wall Street Journal, the *Terre Haute Tribune,* the *Harvard Business Review, The Garrett County Weekly,* to current magazines and books, to respected authorities, and to classical or country philosophers. And do not be afraid to include some original ideas.

Remember that most of us pride ourselves on making decisions and judgments based on logic and analysis. But if you were fully honest about how you selected your car, your house, or your spouse, would you say you decided by using logic alone? We actually make decisions based on a healthy mix of logic, instinct, emotion, political savvy, and sometimes general cussedness. If your presentation appeals to several of these qualities in your listeners, rather than just one, you will be more effective.

Always remember this progression of working backward from the bottom line:

1. Create a powerful closing.

2. Create a rousing opening that captures and directs their attention.

3. Prepare two or three main points.

4. Support those points with a variety of material, making sure that every story, illustration, and example links vitally to the bottom line.

Purpose Determines Structure

There are five main purposes for business presentations. All are designed to move the listener to action, but each has a slightly different intention and focus. We speak to teach, to inform, to inspire, to persuade, or to entertain. Let us explore each of the five with a definition, a general outline, and one specific example.

Purpose 1: To Teach

This presentation sacrifices breadth of topic in order to focus on teaching a specific skill. Most effective in smaller groups (under 35), this presentation includes extensive group participation. Such participation is most valuable in helping to introduce, practice, and apply the new skill. Here is an outline of the teaching presentation:

1. Benefits
2. Elements
3. Illustration or model
4. Group exercise
5. Individual exercise
6. Application

If you were to use this outline to prepare a training session, it might go something like this:

Training for Video-Enhanced Speaking

Benefits

Welcome to our session on 16 feet of face. This session has been designed to prepare you to get up on stage this week here at the convention, knowing that your face is being simulcast in full living color on two giant screens behind you. We will help make you comfortable with the idea that your 12-inch teeth and 16-foot face are coming across powerfully and effectively.

Elements

Here are your ground rules in a nutshell: Know what you do not control, and learn to love your face.

    First, recognize what you do not control. In this special situation, you no longer have to worry about light or sound. Trust the technical experts. We will go onto the stage in a few moments so you can experiment with the sound, feel the lights, and check the height of the microphone. Once you know you can trust the experts in these areas, you need never again tap the microphone or say, "Can everybody hear me?" This time, let the experts take total care of you.

Next, learn to love your face. It is asymmetric, it does funny things as it talks, it is not perfect, it is experienced. Even though you are not going to turn around on stage and watch your giant self, it helps to know that to get yourself beyond face fright. Woody Allen said that you are the only one who does not know what the backs of your ears look like. Strangers on a train or bus have more knowledge than you do about the 360 degrees that make up your head. Loosen up. Get in front of a mirror or video camera, and watch your face make as many movements as possible. Be as animated as you can be. Become more comfortable with your mobile, fascinating face.

A part of learning to love your face is accepting makeup when it is offered. Makeup offers three distinct benefits. First, ironically, it helps you look more natural. Your emotions and the lighting may combine to give you a pale or sallow look. Makeup can restore your natural healthy glow. Second, it adds dimensionality. Makeup emphasizes the dimensions and contours of your face, offsetting the flattening out created by the camera and screen. Third, makeup helps disguise any sweating, so that even on camera you can still look calm, composed, contained, and interested.

Illustration

I would like to invite a male volunteer to come forward for me to demonstrate how we will use powder on you this week. Most women have some past experience with makeup, so it is not as foreign to them. Let us give one of you men some practice . . . . (Volunteer comes up and accepts powder. "How did that feel?" He responds.)

Group Exercise

Closely linked to learning to love your face is selecting the best clothing to wear. In general, avoid red, white, and black since they can bleed, bloom, or fade on camera. Choose gray, blue, bone, beige, or ivory with neutral or pastel shades around your face. Avoid large or vivid prints, bright plaids, stripes, or designs such as herringbone. Each of these may distract from your message. Avoid large metallic jewelry that could reflect lights and bracelets or watches that might make noise. Here are two people dressed very well for video-enhanced speaking. Come on up, Anne Marie and Bud. Now, group, tell me what they are wearing that fits the guidelines you just heard. (Audience responds.)

Individual Exercise
Now, turn to the person next to you and talk for 2 minutes about any tips you plan to apply this week and what you think you will wear on camera. (Audience responds.)

Application
In a moment we will tour the stage and test all the equipment in operation. Are there any more questions here before we have our tour? (Answer some questions.) We will look at some examples of eye contact with the camera while we are on stage.

Here is one reassuring thought for you. Critic Alexander Woolcott once commented on a stage performance he saw: "The scenery in the play was beautiful, but the actors kept getting in front of it." Let us allow this friendly video technology to keep the audience's attention on us and on our ideas to highlight the important messages we have brought to this convention. Let your 16 feet of face say, "Onward to success!"

(Tour the stage, let each one appear on screen, offer tips on eye contact.)

Notice the flexibility of the technical structure—the elements, illustrations, and exercises may be repeated for each skill or tip you wish to present. When the focus is to teach, invest less time in actually delivering the information and more time in exploring and applying it.

Purpose 2: To Inform

This presentation sacrifices the exploration and application in order to include more information. It is appropriate for large groups as well as small. Generally, it follows this pattern:

1. Preview.
2. Key idea 1 and specifics.
3. Key idea 2 and specifics.
4. Key idea 3 and specifics.
5. Here is what this means to you.
6. Here is what you can do about it.

If you were to use this outline to prepare an informational presentation, it might go something like this:

Welcoming Parents to Orientation for First-Year Students

Preview

Welcome, parents and guardians! As you visit us here at Virginia Polytechnic Institute, affectionately known as Virginia Tech, we would like to give you an overview of what you can expect in your son's and daughter's first year at our university. We will look at three areas: academics, housing, and expenses.

(The speaker continues spending a few minutes on each topic and giving detailed specifics in all three areas.) Here are the three topics outlined:

Key Idea 1 and Specifics

I. *Academics*
An overview of the engineering school
Our philosophy
First-year courses
Grade requirements and reports
Resources available

Key Idea 2 and Specifics

II. *Housing*
Policy on first-year housing
Range of dorms and visitation hours
Safety and security
Meals and hours
Laundry
Telephones

Key Idea 3 and Specifics

III. *Expenses*
Personal-computer requirement
Printer optional
Tuition and fees
Dorm fees
Assistance options
Refunds

What It Means to the Audience

What this all means to you is that we recognize and respect the commitment you make in sending your daughters and sons to us for an education. We are partners in creating tomorrow's community. If you have questions or concerns, we will be glad to hear them and to find answers for you.

What the Audience Should Do

As you take your tour of the campus now, reflect on what we have covered today. Our engineering faculty will be in the green lounge of Paradine Hall between 4 and 5 P.M. Come visit with us there at your convenience. Your children are embarking on one of life's great adventures here. Parents and teach-

ers support them in separate ways. Unto this task, I commend us all.

Purpose 3: To Inspire

This presentation is aimed at the audience's natural desire to act, focusing that desire on a current task or project. The goal here is to secure commitment to an idea and to produce results in support of that idea. This topic is appropriate for groups of any size. Generally, it follows this pattern:

1. Current condition
2. Shared vision of a more favorable future
3. Steps to take
4. *You* make the difference
5. Urge to action

An inspirational talk might sound something like this:

Why Come to Sales Seminars?

Current Condition

A salute to all of you who decided to attend our 12th annual sales seminar. There you were—facing the day-to-day demands of calls, contracts, quotas, and follow-ups. Perhaps you asked yourself, "What can I gain from going to the seminar this year?" You looked at your desk, your reports, and your log and said, "Maybe I should stay here and clear up all this paperwork." But you made the decision. You said to yourself, "If I just come away with one great idea . . . " Welcome, we are glad you are here.

Shared Vision of a More Favorable Future

We would like to offer you several great ideas this year, and you will decide which are the ones for you. This program is designed first to refresh your productive focus and make it easier for you to get up and go into the world each day. It is also designed to renew and expand some critical sales skills, to make you a better listener and a better reader of messages from prospects. It will show you how to let the customer help you close the sale. You should leave this seminar refreshed, renewed, and rekindled in your career.

Steps to Take

You have taken the first step. You are here. Congratulations. Step 2 is to set some formal and informal goals for yourself. Think for a moment. "What is it I most need right now?" Define that for yourself as specifically as possible. Do not overlook informal goals. Are there people you have wanted to meet, contacts you have wanted to establish, some healthy exercise you want to continue? Step 3 is to act on the goals. Set a schedule that ensures you productive time to focus on reaching those goals. Then attend the sessions and engage in the activities that support the results you want. Step 4 is to keep an action planning calendar. For every good idea or intention you set at the seminar, define a starting point and a date by which you will do it. Whenever possible, find someone else with an interest in a similar idea and arrange to check in with each other occasionally for progress reports. Commit yourself to taking action. Step 5 is to go home after the seminar and report to colleagues what you learned. Invite them to remind you periodically of your goals.

You Make the Difference

Charles Martin and Bridget Cavarocchi, a retail sales team who attended this seminar last year, sent us this letter about 6 months afterward:

Dear Nick and Kathleen,

Like many at the seminar 6 months ago, we had a great time, felt churned up and raring to go, and gave the session rave reviews. We set three goals for our team and promptly forgot all about them when we faced that desk and telephone on Monday.

Your 2-month reminder letter hit in a lull that allowed us to take a moment to look back and to look forward. Taking out our notebooks to review our action plans, we were surprised to realize we had already achieved one of the goals and were working on the second one. It was almost as if, by resolving to act, we had unconsciously started in that direction and produced great results. Our volume is up 11 percent, and profitability is up 18 percent. The third goal took more specific focus, but the results are now coming in. Be assured, we will see you at the next session.

Urge to Action

Their story and record are typical, possibly even modest compared to what you might do with the ideas you adapt, blend, steal, or create here. You make the difference—in your life, in your job, in your community, in your world. Make that difference. Focus all your attention on your goals for the next few days. Christopher Morley once said, "High heels were invented by a woman who had been kissed on the forehead." Use this conference to invent your own high heels, to position yourself to get the results you want.

Purpose 4: To Persuade

This type of presentation blends information and inspiration to convince the audience of your views. In persuasion, you predict that there will be some objections, and you address them directly to move the audience toward an agreement and a closing action. Although persuasion is appropriate for any size group, it is often most productive when it is used on a board or voting body during deliberations. Generally, persuasion follows this pattern:

1. Current condition

2. Negative and positive futures

3. Key points

4. Undercut objections

5. Desired future

6. Urge to act

A persuasive presentation might sound something like this:

Preparing Employers as Spokespersons

Current Condition

We are facing a crisis in communicating with the public, our customers. People today turn more and more to television for their news. The 45-second clip on the evening news has more impact than all our carefully crafted informative articles in newspapers. Increasingly the person featured on that clip is not someone from headquarters who can give a balanced response to hostile and challenging questions. Sometimes the person featured is an operations manager from a community production facility.

Negative and Positive Futures

Do we want to continue to let our company be represented on the national evening news by unprepared, awkward managers who are good at their technical jobs but unskilled at mastering the media? Or do we want to invest a modest amount of time and money in preparing two people from every facility in basic skills as company spokespersons? They, in turn, can return to their locations and train as many of their people as possible.

Key Points

The proposal in front of you outlines the program I recommend. The one-page summary on top will help me point out key features.

First, the program will be specifically tailored to our industry. We will review video clips of managers who have been interviewed. We will analyze their strengths and how they might have done better.

Second, individual videotaping will help ensure that our new representatives practice and extend their skills. They will be trained in strategies for observing themselves objectively and will learn to be perpetually prepared.

Third, one focus will be on their coaching themselves and others so those managers can go back and prepare their employees.

Undercut Objections

Some of you will object to the costs involved. Let me point out that we spend millions every year in advertising, yet let one fearful, anxious, uncertain manager wipe out the beneficial effects of that advertising in 3 minutes on the nightly news. Consider this small investment an insurance policy for our giant investment in advertising.

Some will ask, "Why does the corporate communication vice-president not become the official and only spokesperson?" The reasons, of course, have to do with timing and public confidence. When an emergency arises in a community, these people want and deserve answers now. Often higher corporate executives are not available at the precise time and place of a crisis, and our managers have the product knowledge necessary to do a good job. All this program will do is train them to focus on giving consumers the accurate information they need. Giving our employees the necessary practice and confidence will ease their awkwardness at being interviewed, which is often misinterpreted as concern about product safety.

Desired Future

The goal of the program is to put meaning behind one of our operating principles. We like to believe that every employee is our public relations representative. This training helps make that principle a reality. It gives people the assurance they need to come across well. It gives our company the strength of a worldwide network of trained spokespersons.

Urge to Act

I welcome your questions, and I propose we consider all factors and accept this proposal today.

Purpose 5: To Entertain

This type of presentation appears to defy all patterns, yet actually conforms loosely to a standard design. The entertaining speech, usually the postbanquet address, uses humor to influence an audience of any size. Once the audience is loosened up, one key idea is presented, still on a light note. *Note:* This is the most difficult of all presentations because it requires great ease and elegance. It is also the most difficult to describe vividly in print because so much depends on the speaker's timing and charisma.

James H. Boren, noted author, businessman, sculptor, and media commentator, is a master at this type of presentation. Dr. Boren's postbanquet talk might include these stages:

1. Warmup
2. Theme 1
3. Theme 2
4. Theme 3
5. One point to remember
6. Cool-down

The Search for the Ultimate Mumble

Warmup
Dr. Boren's warmup would admit to his other major titles, Mr. Mumbles and the Searcher for the Ultimate Mumble. He might describe that his lifelong quest has carried him into many business settings just like this and that "I may be getting close!" During the cocktail hour he heard several people starting to "fuzzify," or "globate" (Boren's verbs). Those activities are sure signs that candidates for the coveted title of Ultimate Mumbler may lurk nearby.

Theme 1
Such candidates, he warns, face heavy competition from gov-ernment and the Bureaucratic Zoo *(one of his books), where people*

orchestrate and dialogue
in words that we adore
The words that we've all mumbled
a million times or more . . .
                    so we can
fingertap together
in a dedicated way
and postpone all decisions
until another day.

Theme 2
Not all mumbling is bad, he admits. It helps you "appear wise while safeguarding the spirit of mental vacuity." "Mar-

ginal thinkers and prodigious ponderers" treasure the thought that "a mumble can never be quoted."

Theme 3

Boren then selects an award winner—some group whose bureaucratic mumbling is in a class by itself. He awards them his hand-sculpted, one-of-a-kind awards—the Order of the Bird. Boren details the sterling and outstandingly dynamic inaction created by the organizational mumbling. The winner is announced at all his public presentations until someone from the organization appears to accept the "bird" in person.

One Point to Remember

No one could play with communication so much, Boren admits, who did not truly love and respect its proper use. Review your own use of language, he reminds audiences. Be sure your language builds action and does not smother it. Defuzzify!

Cool-Down

Otherwise, as you leave here tonight, you can return comfortably to the gray world where "orbital dialogs . . . and steadfast yesbutisms . . . weave the acceptable patterns of decision postponement (with the) pulsating vitality of nondirective logic." Boren might then yawn masterfully, lean forward into the microphone, and whisper quietly, "Help."

The All-Purpose Outline

You may feel that none of these five examples fits your situation. In that case, adapt this all-purpose outline—six organizational rules to help you create your own structure.

Start Where They Are

Your best point of entry with any group is linked to how they are feeling now, today. If they are excited at just having met a major sales or production quota, you could come out bubbling with enthusiasm. But this same rah-rah opening may raise the hackles of people in a more neutral mood. Therefore, try to find a middle ground—choose an opening consistent with your natural style and their current mood.

Focus on Benefits

Help them listen by helping them see the benefits of listening. What will they get out of the skills and information you are offering? Focus primarily not on the company benefits but on the personal benefits, because they are usually what audience members are thinking about.

Offer Direction or Guidelines

This portion of the speech presents well-defined ideas or suggestions related to the action or viewpoint you want them to take.

Include Specifics

Flesh out the directions or guidelines with specifics to reinforce your point.

Relate to Them Personally

In this segment, you challenge your listeners and appeal to the very best in them. You link the proposed actions and expected benefits to a greater vision for the community, the industry, the world.

Urge to Act

Recommend that they take the action which the speech was designed to generate. Implant a timed-release 24-hour reminder, if possible.

The Speech Preparation Checklist

So far you have researched your audience thoroughly, defined your bottom line, and selected the type and purpose of your presentation. What next?

Consider the following preparation checklist. Not everyone completes all steps for each speech. But each step can help you feel totally focused and prepared when that critical challenge comes along.

1. Write out the bottom-line closing. Memorize your last sentence thoroughly.

2. Write out your high-impact opening. Memorize your first sentence thoroughly.

3. Outline your key points.

4. Research or reflect on stories, examples, illustrations, quips, or quotes to accompany the key points.

5. Write out the full text of the speech with all supporting material included. *Or* create a detailed outline of the same content.

6. Present your entire speech out loud. Change any language that is clumsy to pronounce or to listen to. Prepare for the ear before preparing for the eye.

7. Read through again for timing. How long does your delivery take? Do your timed reading at about the pace at which you plan to speak. Then add another 30 percent. For

example, if you time yourself presenting at about 20 minutes, your delivered speech will be closer to 26 minutes in length.

8. Audiotape yourself presenting the text. Listen 3 to 10 times to the tape, over a few days, if possible.

9. Tape yourself again, this time using only brief notes or none at all.

10. Practice several times on tape. Keep the best version, and play that as often as possible as the day of the speech approaches. Occasionally replay only the last 5 minutes so that you are most familiar with your bottom-line closing.

11. Prepare or practice with your visual aids or props. Some people find that these can take the place of an outline.

12. To incorporate your strengths in your next presentation, audiotape the speech itself. Note strengths and areas for development. Notice whether your stories and examples worked and why.

The effort you invest in this preparation process can yield satisfying dividends for you and the audience. Of course, not every speech demands this amount of preparation, and you will not usually have enough time to be so thorough. But it is good to be familiar with a comprehensive approach when a crucial occasion arises.

Opening with Impact and Closing with Direction

How, then, do you prepare the opening and closing? Unfortunately the standard opening is often to thank the introducer, thank the planner, thank the organization, thank the people who set up the chairs, and on and on. One theory is that this gives the audience a chance to settle down. This is not necessarily so. It often gives them time to get restless. The opener of the meeting or conference may appropriately welcome attendees. After that official welcome, however, successful speakers generally plunge right into their speeches, still paying attention to the "start from where they are" principle.

The Introduction—A Framework

One key element of your speech, which is often overlooked, is the introduction of you as speaker. Yes, you should prepare it yourself. It is part of your presentation. Send a copy—triple-spaced, orator type or all capitals, no more than 2 pages—to the meeting planner or the person who will introduce you. Tell that person clearly whether you want it presented exactly as written or whether she or he is welcome to change it to better match the traditional introductions. Bring an extra copy or two with you, just in case the introducer fails to arrive. You can, in an emergency, draft someone from the audience 10 minutes before you begin.

The introduction should last 1 to 2 minutes—no longer. Its purpose is to set the stage for your presentation. This introduction, therefore, satisfies the audience's unconscious curiosity about why this is the right speaker on the right topic at the right time for the right audience. Here is a sample of such an introduction:

Introduction of David Miller

Here to speak to us today about "Creativity and the Bottom Line" is Dr. David Miller, coproducer of a recent public broadcasting system teleconference on this subject and president of The Phoenix Company, which specializes in organizational effectiveness. The exploration of creativity was a key thread running through Dave's work at the Marriott Corporation and at Amtrak, where he was manager of human resource development.

In his 22 years of varied professional experience, Dave has channeled group and individual creativity into on-the-job improvements for increased effectiveness. He is especially noted for documenting and training in the creative process so that clients can observe their own progress and coach themselves in creativity on their own.

Dave earned his master's degree in physics and his doctorate in human resource development. He is active in civic and professional groups. Most notably, he chairs The American Society for Training and Development National Research Committee, which is charged with giving an outlet to the best and the brightest ideas in research on productivity and effectiveness.

If our industry is to meet the complex challenges of international competition and the changing economic environment, we need to harness the creative resources of our people.

Here to help us turn our ideas into effective action is Dr. Dave Miller (lead applause).

The Opening

You can almost imagine the reaction to such an introduction. People sit a little straighter in their chairs and turn up their listening equipment. Now the speaker must open with power. Picture Dave Miller after such an introduction. He approaches the podium, looks out at an array of expectant faces during 10 glowing seconds of silence, and says:

"Six inches to success, 6 inches to improved performance, 6 inches to applied creativity . . . these inches pave our way to profits and productivity. And where are these 6 inches? Between the ears of every person in our organization. Now let us talk about putting those 6 inches to work . . . ."

The Closing

Let us skip to Dave's closing; as was recommended earlier, he ends with a reference to the opening:

"So those are the principles for putting creativity to work. First, recognize that everyone has creative capability. Second, create an environment where creativity can flourish. Third, adapt group processes to harness creativity. Fourth, reward creative accomplishments.

    Next time you round the cloverleaf entrance or exit on a highway, think of the lives and dollars that have been saved by the improved safety and speed of limited-access highways with overpasses. Remember that some person or team created that idea. Think about the vital contribution they made to our lives. Think of all the other contributions still waiting to be made. Think of the resources in our field—the people who are ready, willing, and able to create those contributions.

Next time you look into the face of a colleague, think about the tremendous 6 inches of talent lying, waiting to be tapped, behind those eyes. Decide now on the first step you will take to put that talent—and your own—to greater use. Let us explore inner space. Let us harness creativity for success, and let us do it now."

Improving Your Audience's Listening Pattern

Remember, people listen at the beginning of the speech to "get the drift." After a bit, their attention may wander. Once they sense the closing coming, they tune in again. An awkward or lukewarm opening only increases the chances of your losing their attention. And a weak closing leaves them wondering why they bothered to listen at all.

Remember your reaction when you heard a speaker close, "Well, my time is up and that is about all I have to say. I guess I will sit down." Such a closing wastes the moment of optimum attention.

So how can you help people listen better and minimize their moments of distraction? How can you change the natural pattern of attention at the beginning and end, with resting in between, to a better pattern—one with peaks of good listening regularly throughout the presentation and very *brief* rests in between?

Listening Patterns

The primary secret to holding attention is to vary the predictable. Pique audience interest with variety and specificity. As the audience's attention starts to lag, drag a surprise word or reference across the edge of their awareness. They will blink, say to themselves, "What am I hearing?" and be with you again for a while.

Depending on the time of day and the type of function and audience, you may want to program these "pique points" about every 5 to 7 minutes. Here are some effective strategies to grab attention:

1. Start one section of your talk with a variation on the statement "Here is what this will mean to every person in this room over the next year." This is a specific summons to your listeners. Enlightened self-interest is one of the strongest motivations for careful listening.

2. Tell a story. People listen well to stories—especially those with a lot of concrete, sensory detail. Help them travel to a specific time and place with recognizable sights, sounds, smells, tastes, and textures. Involve them in painting their own version of your word picture. Tie the story to a key point in your presentation.

3. Use a powerful or humorous quotation. A vivid quote or quip can embed a nugget of information in the minds of listeners. This helps them remember and act on what you say. Remember Ronald Reagan's quip in the second 1984 debate with Presidential candidate Walter Mondale. In his response to the moderator's question "Is age an issue in this campaign?" Reagan, then 73, reversed the tone of a previously lackluster debate by replying, "I refuse to hold my opponent's youth and inexperience against him."

4. Show props or visual aids. These devices will also reawaken listener attention; they illustrate or support your

LISTENING PATTERNS

(30 minute speech)

A. Usual Pattern

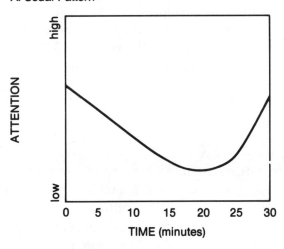

B. Planned Pattern

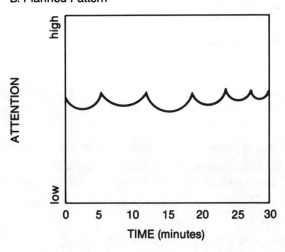

message while making it more concrete. Be sure, however, that any such display can be seen from all parts of the room.

5. Put speech rhythm and parallel repetition to work for you. People like to listen to series of threes. They also like to hear variations and repetitions. Most memorable speakers use this fact in their favor. Take, for instance, Lincoln's strong use of parallel prepositions in "government of the people, by the people and for the people"; John F. Kennedy's balance in "let us never negotiate out of fear, but let us never fear to negotiate"; and Adlai Stevenson's rhythmic wit in "A diplomat's life is made up of three ingredients: protocol, Geritol, and alcohol."

6. Occasionally, be dramatic. Used sparingly and in the appropriate context, drama can make your presentation stronger. Dropping your voice to a whisper or raising it to a shout gets attention quickly. Putting people through a whole speech of voice gymnastics, however, may just exhaust them and you. Grand or sweeping gestures may also be appropriate now and then. Drama is like salt in a recipe—a little bit adds flavor and spice but too much calls attention only to itself and not to the dish.

7. Involve the audience. Probably the least used and most potentially effective attention-keeping strategy is audience participation. Yes, of course, they are involved as long as they are listening. But you can involve them on at least two other levels. Ask them for a show of hands in response to a question, or ask them to look up at the ceiling and start to see there a picture of a newspaper headline they would like to see as a result of the action you are urging them to take. The second level of involvement is interaction. After they have "seen" their headline goal, they sit and talk to the person next to them, discussing their headlines for a moment or two.

THE A.M./P.M. FACTOR

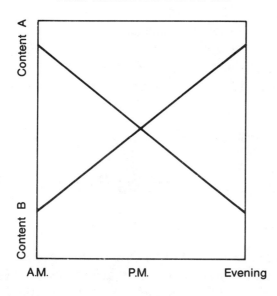

The LRA Test

Some business people dismiss these attention strategies, saying, "They are fine for revivals and rallies, but not for the real world." But remember, your highest responsibility as a speaker is to help the audience *listen, remember,* and *act* on what you say—the LRA test. It is better to be slightly less dignified and meet that responsibility than to stay safely formal and lose your listeners. The key is to accommodate your strategies to the topic, this particular audience, and your natural style and skills.

The A.M.-P.M. Factor

Most people listen better in the morning, and the quality of their listening declines during the day. So, in an all-day seminar, it is wiser to consider starting the day with a mix of 75 percent information analysis and statistics (content A) and 25 percent stories, humor, illustrations, and involvement exercises (content B). In the afternoon, you might use about 50 percent each of content A and content B. And in the evening, use 25 percent of content A and 75 percent of content B. If you have one hour-long speech to deliver and it is full of content A, try to schedule it as early in the day as possible.

Telling People Things They Do Not Want to Hear

Business presenters often have to deliver unpleasant messages. You have to tell people that their budget has been cut; that regulations have changed, requiring more paperwork; that a project went over schedule and the bonus they hoped to share has been eliminated. We often approach such a chore with a more apologetic tone than is necessary. In fact, such a tone may only aggravate the situation. The way to break unpleasant news is swiftly and directly. You might open such a presentation in this way:

"My message today is one you will not want to hear and I do not want to deliver. But it is important to face the reality and get on with our lives. The rumors of the past week are true: As of the close of business Friday, our company is closing its doors. There will be pain, anger, grief, fear, and frustration for all of us. Our purpose here this morning is to put those feelings aside for a few moments and tell you about details affecting you in that closing."

Give people the toughest news first. Give them details as openly and accurately as is appropriate. Name and acknowledge their feelings. Focus attention productively on solutions rather than on blame. Offer encouragement and support. Give people an acceptable outlet for their feelings. Close with a hopeful, yet realistic message.

It is a sure mark of professional maturity when you feel fully capable of delivering bad news. You have reached the point when you recognize that people do not have to like you to respect your message, that they do not have to like you to benefit constructively from what you say. But do exercise some caution. Remember that some people associate the message with the messenger. Ask yourself if there might be violent reactions from people in the group. Take precautions for your own and the group's safety.

Key Ideas

- The substance or content of your speech is determined by your purpose, not by how much you know about the subject.
- Start preparing content by deciding what you want people to do or think as a result of listening (bottom-line results).
- Select your structure based on your intention to teach, inform, inspire, persuade, or entertain.
- Adapt the 12-step preparation process to your needs.
- Prepare your own introduction.
- Open with impact; close with direction.
- Use seven strategies to help improve your audience's listening patterns.
- Deliver bad news swiftly and directly.

CHAPTER SIX

The Style Side of the Coin

The High-Impact Approach

The fourth element in the SASS formula is style—the way in which you deliver your presentation. This includes everything from the way you harness your stress energy to a secret for ending on time. We talked earlier about your natural, personal style, and that is an important ingredient here. But, again, that style can and should be tailored for different occasions and purposes.

Picture this scene: Your introduction as speaker has just ended. You rise and walk briskly toward the lectern. You pause to establish eye contact and recognize your notes on the stand. You smile and open powerfully with the microphone at perfect height and volume. Your voice is authoritative, yet lilting with zest and passion. Your flow is logical yet compelling. You present your key points and simultaneously tailor a few of your comments and allusions to today's events, either for this group or in the news. Your gestures come effortlessly and unconsciously from your message. Your voice is varied in pitch and volume, adding additional texture and color to your comments. You finish with a glowing sense of purpose, knowing you have effected a call to action or a change of heart. After a respectful few seconds of silence, the audience explodes into applause. You smile, wave, and walk off. They are impressed and plan to take your recommended action.

An Effective Contrast

Suppose, however, that this high-impact person is not you, but rather the speaker you must follow on the program. Although your natural style is similar to what you have just seen, you decide to vary your style a bit to give the listeners a break from all that dynamic supercharge. After your introduction, you approach the lectern more deliberately. You ask them to close their eyes for a moment and go on a mental journey to the last time (your topic) was important to them. How did that situation look, feel, and sound? After a couple of deep, relaxing breaths, they open their eyes again. You then present your information in a relaxed, deliberate, gentle progression. Voice variety and gestures are on a smaller scale, yet natural and in proportion to your subject. Your closing asks them to take that mental journey again. This time they see themselves as having accomplished the action you are recommending. They are now basking in its benefits. How does this look, feel, and sound? How do they feel about their accomplishments? Give them 2 minutes to share their journey experiences with a partner. Your closing is quietly inspirational. Their focus is still heavily introverted, and the applause is polite and gentle, almost unconscious. This audience is empowered and will likely take the action step you recommend.

Which Is Better?

The ideal range of your natural style would support you equally well in either type of presentation. The person who can be calm, rational, and reasonable in the board room and dramatic, dynamic, and compelling on stage has the advantage over people with less versatility. Such a flexible person can also elect to be calm, rational, and reasonable on stage and dramatic, dynamic, and compelling in the board room when the situation requires. Each style and several between can be enormously effective. Each has areas of effectiveness in common, and each can be marred by presentation snags.

The Take-Charge Opening

You begin your presentation the moment you are introduced. You have probably seen speakers who, upon being introduced, stopped eating chocolate parfait dessert, reached into a briefcase for notes, stumbled toward the platform, approached the lectern, patted themselves to find their glasses, put the glasses on, looked around to find out how to lower the microphone, cleared their throats, sipped some water, adjusted the glasses again, opened their notes, looked down, and began their presentation on strategic planning with an apology for being caught off guard.

This 13-step symphony of incompetence is an insult to the audience. Only three or four of those steps are necessary. Each additional one saps attention and energy from your message. Here are some tips to streamline your opening process:

- Have everything you need on your person or previously positioned on the lectern or a table nearby. This

includes notes, glasses, water, visual aids, props, anything you will use during the speech. If your notes are
on the lectern, be sure they are clearly marked in a
distinctive or personalized folder, so your introducer
does not remove them accidentally. It may be appropriate to have a duplicate set of notes in your briefcase.

• Stand a few paces away as your are introduced. This
lets you get safely out of your chair before you are in
the spotlight, and it cuts down on the opening time. It
also lets you take several deep and/or short breaths just
before you go on.

• Consider using a battery-operated wireless microphone. This allows you to glide easily into your presentation, confident that your preselected volume level
is perfect. The microphone is clipped to your lapel, tie,
or scarf. The battery clips to a belt or waistband or fits
neatly into a pocket. Such a microphone also ensures
that you do not have to adjust the height, and it gives
you the flexibility to move without sacrificing sound.

A second alternative is the lapel, or lavalier, microphone. This small, sensitive microphone also clips to
your clothing. Unlike the battery-operated model, however, this one is wired to the sound system. A short
wire may keep you more stationary than you wanted,
and a long wire may trip you or become distractingly
tangled. Even so, the lapel microphone allows you to
get out from behind the barrier that is the lectern and
be more visually a part of your message.

If a fixed microphone at the lectern is your only option, try to prearrange the microphone to match your
height. Ideal placement of a fixed microphone is 6 to 8
inches in front of you and 1 to 2 inches below your
chin. This placement allows you to speak across the
top of the microphone, protecting you from the explod-
ing breath of letters such as T and P and the hiss of S.
Such placement also lets your whole face be visible
and expressive rather than hidden behind the equipment.

Many people mistakenly believe that if they can get
by without a microphone, that this will seem more
"natural." You should use a microphone if one is avail-

able and request one if it is needed. There may be hearing-impaired people in your audience. Remember people's tendency to drift away. The microphone keeps you in control, allows you to speak naturally or softly for emphasis, and offers tremendously important crowd control. Follow this rule of thumb: Use a microphone in any group of more than 125 people, if a majority of the audience are over 50 years old, if the room layout requires crowd control, and if your voice is strained.

- Be conscious of your height. If at least 18 inches of your head and shoulders are not easily visible from the audience seating, take action. Do not gauge this from your own point of view on stage. Have someone sit in one of the first three rows and tell you if the height of the stage and the height of the lectern block the view of your face. If this is a problem, move away from the lectern, stand beside it, or have a step stool in place that you can stand on. If you work away from the lectern, you can place your notes on a small table nearby.

- Select cooperative clothing. Do not let your appearance argue with your message. Wear clothes that are appropriate to the occasion and help keep you visible. Find your own best selections based on body type and coloring. Here are some visual realities to consider:

    You may wish to dress like your audience or one degree more formally. If your session is in a resort area and short sleeves are the style, you will fit well in a blazer, less well in a three-piece suit. If you are in Singapore, right on the equator, your Harris tweed wool suit will make both you and the audience itchy. If the setting is formal, select formal clothes.

    Color is important, too. Do you know the color of the stage background? Try not to blend too perfectly, or you will fade away. But also try not to clash strikingly, or people will listen less well. Dark suits with light shirts or blouses are great in two ways. The light material in the V wedge nearest your face focuses attention there. Such suits also tend to have a slimming effect. The disadvantage to dark clothing is that your body can "disappear." Your arms are hard to distinguish, so people miss some of your visual dynamics. Light suits and dresses are great because they draw light and attention to you. They help your whole body reinforce your message visually. They can, however, be distracting if they make you look heavy.

Finally, be sure to choose clothing that is roomy and moves anywhere you need to move. That old favorite jacket, shirt, or blouse might rip noisily as you gesture during your speech. The waistband you are stuffed into can be more on your mind than the critical issue you are here to present. Be comfortable and able to move with confidence.

- Establish eye contact immediately and smile, if appropriate, before you begin to speak. Some nervous starters plunge in before they even take the microphone. Avoid this awkward error. Stand silently for the first 6 seconds to heighten audience expectation about your message.

- Begin speaking. Deliberately choose your voice's pace and pitch to soothe or stimulate the group. Many people start at a pitch slightly higher than normal because they are nervous or enthusiastic. Why not try starting just below your normal pitch and at a slightly slower pace than usual? It is sometimes better to lure or invite the audience in than to hit them over the head.

You have now successfully started. So on to the next challenge: presentation dynamics.

Presentation Dynamics

To keep the audience with you, you have five elements under your control: eye contact, voice variety, gestures and movement, the deliberate use of silence, and visual aids external to your person.

Eye Contact

Two forms of eye contact are particularly ineffective. The first is called "hair"; the second, "bob and flutter." "Hair" occurs when the top of your head is all the audience sees. This posture is used by people reading an unfamiliar text word for word or by people so timid they pretend to be reading even when they have no text. "Bob and flutter" occurs when the speaker afflicted with "hair" ventures to look up with infrequent, disjointed glances at the audience while turning pages in midsentence.

There are four effective forms of eye contact, of which the last three should make up 90 percent of your presentation: *glance, room quarters, sweep,* and *stay.* Glance occurs when the speaker, though reading from a text, has practiced enough to look up periodically for full phrases, sentences, or stories. Room quarters occurs when the speaker has mentally drawn invisible lines back to front and side to side along the room, quartering the room. Having set these quarters, the speaker consciously addresses all four areas periodically, so that no group gets left out of eye contact. With sweep eye contact, the speaker scans a row in a horizontal movement, reaching many people briefly.

Stay occurs when the speaker maintains contact with one person for 6 seconds or one sentence, whichever is longer. This is one of the most effective, yet neglected types of eye contact. Focusing attention on individuals helps the whole audience feel that you are right there with them. It affords the speaker the luxury of reading a few faces every minute in greater depth. One caution: Do *not* pick the people sitting with crossed arms and a furious frown. They may be part of the 2 percent who want you to fail, or they may be just back from oral surgery. Choose instead the ones who smile, nod, or look interested. They will help build your presentation energy.

By the way, there are two other eye contact strategies that do not seem to work. One is the old rule you learned in eighth grade: If you do not want to look into their eyes, look about 6 inches over their heads. Try that in a real audience, and people wonder who the taller people are behind them that you seem to keep addressing. Others have suggested that you can overcome your fear by imagining that everyone in the audience is sitting there nude or in underclothes. With all the other things on your mind, that is a fantasy that might blur your focus—or worse yet, cause an uncontrollable snicker.

Voice

The second presentation element under your control is voice. This includes both your physical production of sound and your style of shaping and using that sound. We already considered that your voice was learned from your family and others in your environment. You learned your rate, pitch, tone, volume, pronunciation, and articulation from the people around as you first started to speak. We usually retain those original qualities unless we make a conscious effort later to speak differently. This explains why people immigrating in their youth can easily keep an accent all their lives. Let us take a closer look at the seven primary qualities of voice.

• *Rate.* The speed at which you speak is your rate. The average rate of speaking is 125 to 150 words per minute. John F. Kennedy was famous for gusts near 400 words per minute. Your own rate may vary in public speaking, so why not clock yourself in a natural conversation with one person or on the telephone? Then clock yourself giving a speech. Your rate should match your purpose. A solemn, formal announcement should be delivered slowly. An excited salute to award winners might be delivered quickly.

An angry outburst may be fast and frightening or slow and menacing.

• *Pitch.* The second aspect of your voice to consider is pitch. Hearing themselves on audiotape or videotape, people often complain that they sound nothing like that unfamiliar voice they are hearing. They are most surprised by the pitch of their voices. Pitch is merely the musical note at which you utter a sound. Higher pitches are associated with excitement, nervousness, anger, femininity, helplessness, or enthusiasm. Lower pitches are associated with threat, deliberateness, manliness, control, or rationality. The middle or average pitches are more neutral—and more boring. Your natural pitch blends notes at many levels. Do not flatten that natural variety for a speech. Let your normal, typical lilt and "music" come through. Beware, though, of the high, nervous voice. It can easily become shrill and annoying to your listeners. Relax your throat and breathing to let your natural pitch emerge.

• *Tone.* Tone blends nasality, resonance, and breath support. Do you produce your sounds in the roundness of a widely open mouth or in the restricted passages of your nose? Is your breath supporting those sounds deeply from the diaphragm or shallowly from your upper chest? Are you supporting each sound with enough breath to add color and texture to your tone? Powerful and effective speakers use breath and sound in the same way singers do. You may, therefore, want to go to a voice or singing coach for one or two sessions on proper breath support and sound production. You do not necessarily need to practice singing, but you can learn exercises to help reshape your breathing and improve your pitch and tone.

• *Volume.* Volume relates closely to tone and breath support. It is, simply, the loudness with which you speak. Experiment with loud and soft volume to build voice variety, so you can underline your message and keep people listening.

• *Pronunciation*. Pronunciation involves your selection and production of sounds that, strung together, make up your way of delivering language. Pronunciation offers us a paradox. Most guidelines recommend a homogeneous middle-American, "white bread" kind of pronunciation. Yet we are regularly delighted with and sometimes even impressed by people with accents. Sometimes we appreciate the accents just because of their novelty. On a panel of experts, the comments of someone with an understandable accent tend to be remembered better than those of others.

What does this paradox mean to you? If you have an accent and can be easily understood by most people, do not completely homogenize your pronunciation. If you were born into a heritage of standard pronunciation, you will just have to develop other techniques for being remembered.

• *Articulation*. Articulation is a much neglected area in voice quality today. Articulation is the clear rendering of sounds, crisply produced and carefully completed. Articulation is the opposite of mumbling and taking sound shortcuts. To say crisply, "I am going to" rather than "O'm gonna" is articulation. To pronounce the final T in contract is articulation. To give each syllable its time and tongue is articulation. Mumbling is the mark of a lazy mind and a lazy mouth. Watch out for such laziness in your speaking.

Movement and Gestures

These are the third element at your command. They tell the audience a great deal about how comfortable you are at speaking and how confident you are in your message. When you stand rigidly behind the lectern and grip the top with white knuckles, you telegraph fear or lack of confidence to your audience. Gestures and motions harmonious to your message give you greater credibility. The audience is extremely sensitive to such movement.

According to Suzy Sutton, a respected media consultant, one area the audience notices first, though unconsciously, is the upper arm, from elbow to shoulder. Stop to think—this is an area of great vulnerability. When a performer raises both arms in an outstretched V at the end of a selection, the message is "please applaud now." The vulnerability is great because the risk of humiliation is great if the audience should fail to respond appropriately. That may be why the nervous speaker keeps the upper arm area less mobile, with elbows almost clenched toward the waist.

The comfortable speaker, though, relaxes this area and moves the full arm in gestures. Observe yourself on videotape and see how you use this critical area. And do not forget about your legs and feet—you do not have to stay glued to that lectern.

Deliberate Use of Silence

This element is an extremely powerful communication device. In an experiment done at the Smithsonian Museums in Washington, D.C., a few years ago, one group of tour guides was instructed to offer the usual tour information but, during the question-and-answer periods, to wait in silence for 6 to 10 seconds before they accepted comments or questions. At first the silences were uncomfortable, the guides reported, but then people asked better questions, ones they had considered more deeply. The discussions were livelier and more satisfying. The volunteer guides were happier and stayed with the assignment longer. Silence worked to invite thoughtful deliberation.

Although as a public speaker you are not necessarily a tour guide, you can learn to employ pause and silence to great advantage. The thoughtful pause after a question or before a key idea can stir or renew audience interest. Effective use of silence is also a mark of mastery in a speaker.

Notice how this element is used by others. Experiment with it for yourself.

Visual Aids External to Your Person

Such devices can underline your message in the eyes and minds of listeners. You can call forth people in the room as visual aids or use props or displays to help make ideas more concrete. You can also use one of the three most common visual technologies—easel pad, transparencies, or slides. Each type is appropriate for certain groups and settings. All effective visual aids share three common characteristics.

1. They are visible to all parts of the room.
2. They include images as well as words.
3. They are completely readable.

The easel pad or flipchart is good because it can be prepared ahead of time or generated on the spot. It is usually best suited to groups of fewer than 50 people because it is hard to read from a distance. However, because it faces the audience, the speaker's back is toward the group when writing, unless he or she has an assistant or a volunteer from the audience make the notations.

Transparencies are shown on an overhead projector. These can also be prepared ahead of time or generated on the spot. They are suited for larger audiences because they can be projected with clear resolution onto a large screen. Lettering on a transparency should be readable to the naked eye at 10 feet away. Use no more than six words to a line and six lines to a page. Illustrations as well as words come across well. One additional advantage of the overhead projector is that you can face the audience as you speak. And, unlike slides, overhead projectors work well in a fully lighted room. On both transparencies and slides, it is better to use light letters against a dark background.

Slides are the most polished and professional visual aid. They allow you to mix words, drawings, and graphs with images of people, equipment, or locations. They are usually more colorful than other types of aids and are of good enough quality for large-screen projection to large groups. You can face the audience while using slides. Their main disadvantage is that they must be shown on a darkened screen area. In some settings this means the entire room must be darker than you would like.

Other sophisticated visual technologies are emerging, including remote-control overhead transparencies and continuously painted computer-generated images. Unfortunately, these are not yet universally available.

Ending on Time

There is one additional presentation dynamic that deserves a heading all to itself. This is ending on time. Let us look at how you do that.

Most basically, you must know at what time you are expected to finish, and you must have a way of keeping an eye on the time while you are speaking. The meeting coordinator can tell you at what time you are scheduled to finish, so that part is easy. Then there are several ways to keep track of time within your session. The best way is to bring a small travel clock and place it on the lectern. For under $25 you can buy one with a built-in stopwatch function. This makes it easier for you to pace yourself through a straight 20-minute segment, rather than worry about ending at exactly 10:48 because you started at 10:28. The audience will not notice you keeping time as you glance now and then at the lectern. If you glance at your watch, though, you may make them uncomfortably aware of the time.

Next best is to be lucky enough to work in a room with an easily visible clock. Do not trust this important element to luck.

A third technique is to glance at your watch occasionally and unobtrusively. The watch may be on your wrist or on the lectern. For the reason stated above, this method is not ideal—but it is better than nothing.

Why do we put such emphasis on time awareness? Because adrenaline generated by speaking often distorts the speaker's time. Time may stretch or compress for you, and your usual awareness disappears. Think back in your life to moments of great fear, joy, risk, or challenge. Remember how time stopped or rushed by. People often experience a similar distortion while speaking. Do not drag your captive audience into your own personal time warp. Also, no matter how many times you rehearsed and timed your speech beforehand, nervousness or external intrusions may alter your pace significantly.

Once you have achieved time awareness, you need flexibility of content. It is a part of your unwritten contract with the audience to convey to them the main ideas you have come to deliver. So the 5-minute version of your half-hour speech would still retain this outline:

1. Benefits-based opening

2. Brief summary of key points

3. Action closing with reference for more complete information

The key points would be introduced, but you would reduce the number of illustrations or examples. Do not be a slave to the 15 visual aids you so carefully prepared. Show the most critical three. It is good to provide the audience with more access to you later. Suggest they join you at the coffee break tomorrow in the northwest corner of the room or call you at the office to explore ideas further. As you develop ease at using the time accordian, you will notice that you can begin to gauge unconsciously when to cut or expand material.

The Question-and-Answer Quandary

QUESTION: Why worry about the question-and-answer period of a speech?

ANSWER: Many people who seek speech coaching want to learn to "think on their feet." They want to be adept at handling questions and answers. They have a great fear that clumsiness in this part of the program will cancel a previously powerful speech. And it can.

QUESTION: If question-and-answer sessions are tough, why agree to them at all?

ANSWER: If the topic is complex or timely, this part of the program invites the audience to seek clarification or updating. It also allows for audience participation and presentation variety in this part of the program. Author and speaker Jeff Davidson says, "The speech is my agenda; the question period is their agenda." The question period also allows you time flexibility in preparing the main part of your talk. A planned 20-minute question period can easily be cut to 5 minutes if your presentation runs over.

QUESTION: Are there cautions to using a question period?

ANSWER: Yes, there are three. First, if there is a great deal of hostility or resistance to the message, the question period can provide time for either a healthy emotional release or a dangerous public attack. Use your best political and emotional judgment here.

Second, if the group is larger than 250 people, you start to lose your audience. They leave or tune out. Question sessions are most productive in groups of under 100 in which everybody can see and hear both questioner and responder.

Third, if your group contains a number of people who like to get up and pronounce judgment or market themselves instead of asking questions, they can make your life miserable, or at least awkward. Learn to interrupt after 12 seconds of an obvious nonquestion by saying, "And your question is . . . ?" If the audience member does not produce an immediate question, call on someone else.

QUESTION: If the group is gigantic, resistant, or rampantly egocentric, are there alternatives to the traditional question period?

ANSWER: Yes. First, you can have blank cards available for each area or row. Participants write questions on cards, which are then collected by ushers and brought to you. You or an assistant may select the questions that will let you reinforce the point you came there to make or that give you the opportunity to address legitimate challenges. One great advantage here is that the questions are brief and do not give the asker a soapbox to speak from.

Another choice is to write certain questions yourself and call on your own questioners. This can sometimes be embarrassing if the audience suspects a plot, so why not tell them there is a plot and be dramatic about calling on the planted questions? This method is sometimes effective in getting the group warmed up to ask questions of their own.

Finally, you can tell them that because of the size of the group or the time allowed, you have decided to conduct a different kind of question-and-answer session. You are going to answer the three kinds of questions you are asked most often after this presentation. You then conduct a question-and-answer period with yourself.

QUESTION: What is my most productive focus when answering?

ANSWER: Keep your focus on the group as a whole and the message you are there to deliver. Do not get dragged off onto the personal tangent or crusade of someone in the audience.

QUESTION: What tips are there for answering hostile questions?

ANSWER: Restate, reframe, reply honestly and briefly, and then move on. Restate the question in nearly the same language used by the questioner. Then reframe the question to link it to your message or to apply more generally to your audience. Reply honestly and briefly. Do not be afraid to say, "I do not have the answer to that question right now. If you will write that question on the back of your business card or a piece of paper, I will get back to you on it next week." Do not be afraid to use quotes or to be humorous. Move on briskly to the next person.

Here is an example of an employee questioning management at the annual full-staff meeting. The speaker has correctly assessed that the group is ready to adjourn, and the resident complainer asks a question. The speaker restates, reframes, and replies briefly with a softening touch of humor.

EMPLOYEE QUESTION We heard your product goals, but when are we gonna get a shorter workweek?

YOUR REPLY

- Restate. *"You are asking when you will get a shorter workweek."*
- Reframe. *"In other words, you are saying that the goals of job security, raises, and benefits should be expanded to include options for more leisure time."*
- Reply. *"The answer is, 'Not this year.' But look at the good side. Susan Ertz said, 'Millions long for immortality who do not know what to do with themselves on a rainy Sunday afternoon.' For at least one more year, an excess of leisure time is not a problem we will have to deal with!"*
- Move on. *"Next question."*

QUESTION: Is there any all-purpose escape-hatch answer to truly embarrassing questions?

Here is one that often works. Look directly at the questioner and say, "Why do you ask that question?" In revealing motives or offering clarification, the asker often defuses the challenge and gives you valuable time to think.

QUESTION: What is the biggest trap to avoid in question-and-answer sessions?

ANSWER: That trap is the failure to take the floor again, as speaker, to deliver an action-oriented powerful closing. Remember, optimum listening is available to you right at the end of a session. If you close with "Well, that is all we have time for, good luck," you will have wasted that optimum opportunity. Take back your role as formal presenter for 1 to 3 minutes at the closing after the questions and answers. As strategic marketing specialist Peter Johnson assures us, you owe it to your audience—and to your message.

Overcoming Opening Panic

"Hundreds of people sat there waiting to applaud or attack. I started my speech, looked out over the tapestry of faces. My surface continued to speak and smile, but my subterranean depths were in panic. Panic won! Five seconds into the most critical speech of my early career, I fainted."

An executive, very successful today, gives this account of starting out many years ago. Few of us have had quite so dramatic a beginning, but we may have experienced our own version of stage fright. Let us look at another example of panic in action and consider some essentials that can replace panic with poise.

"My trouble was platforms—getting on them and staying on them. At one important motivational presentation, I had rehearsed my entry as I always do, a regular part of my preparation. Unfortunately, the introducer did too good a job. His ringing words fired me up, and I decided to run from my seat and leap onto the stage. Well, I leapt, skidded on my right heel, slipped halfway to my left knee, recovered, and walked the rest of the way to stage front and center."

This speaker suffered from a different form of opening panic—an excess of zeal, a desire to be spectacular and unforgettable. While this desire often leads happily to a high-energy presentation, it can also, as we saw here, lead to some problems, even dislocated body parts.

There are many other symptoms of opening panic: the high-pitched voice, shallow breath, rushed speech, averted eyes, tight posture, and disjointed gestures. These are signals to us and to our audience that the panic is taking over.

The best treatment for panic is prevention. Yes, there are ways to treat panic:

Know Your Platform Completely

Chuck Waterman, cofounder of the communications consulting firm Speak/Write, advised that you "walk up to your platform from every possible point of entry and egress. Look for things that could trip you up on the way there and everywhere on the platform you could possibly move to. Get the *feel* of the place and your relationship to it."

Prepare Your Primary Equipment

Your body, voice, and energy should be as carefully prepared as you would prepare your technical support. Do not neglect food or sleep. The best support technology will not make up for speakers who are careless with their primary equipment—themselves.

Know What Your Audience Expects

Speaker and author Jim Cathcart says that we gain our audience's trust more easily if we harmonize with those expectations (Tony Alessandra and Jim Cathcart, *The Business of Selling,* Reston Press, 1984). How would you respond, for example, to a psychotherapist who kept a pet tarantula on her desk? Expectations influence trust.

Approach the Platform with Presence and Poise

"Imagine you are a 1000-watt light bulb," advises noted Toastmaster Mary Kennedy. "When your time comes, just turn on those thousand watts, march up to the front, let everyone feel the brilliance of your light for a few seconds as you look around the room. Then start your presentation. You will find that everyone is with you."

Develop Confidence

Develop the confidence in your material and in your delivery that comes only with thorough preparation. People in your audience are investing their precious time by being there. They want you to succeed. Help them!

Remember, few people are entirely successful at replacing panic with poise at all times. When lapses occur, accept them and learn from them. So far you have not fainted in front of a group. And if you did, it would make a great story someday!

Subduing Stress Symptoms

The symptoms of speaker's stress and opening panic are all too familiar to most of us. You may experience any of or all the following: dry mouth, shallow breathing, shrill voice, queasy stomach, rushed speech, wooden posture, and inability to make eye contact. There are two ways to combat these symptoms. First, you can become experienced enough at handling different groups that you rarely experience these feelings in the extreme. Second, you can find a message you care enough about to let it be more important to you than fear.

A good speech is one where the speaker has a message; a great speech is one where the message has a speaker. When you find yourself the advocate of a significant message you care deeply about, turn yourself over to that message. Make yourself less the center of attention. You are a conduit to channel this message to these listeners. Once you are not the focus, you will find it easier to relax.

Do not be daunted by the serious-sounding idea of finding a message so important to you. It can be at the level of defending home, family, nation, courage, love, or another major life force. But it can also be at a much less dramatic level. Is there not something in your career or industry that you feel passionately enough about to let it become a life theme or a speaking theme for you for perhaps a year or two? Find a subject you feel strongly enough about, and it will teach you all you need to know about yourself and audiences.

Both these solutions take a while. In the meantime, perhaps what you really wanted was a magic pill.

An Easy Out?

There is a magic pill, but do you really want to take it? Inderol, available by prescription, blocks adrenaline and allows a speaker to remain relaxed. After consultation with your doctor about possible side effects, you might decide you would like to try it. Experts advise against it. There is one nonmedical side effect you should consider—you may be relaxed enough to be thoroughly boring.

Welcome your butterflies. Make them right at home. Adrenaline can be an asset. It can give you that touch of fire, that sense of focused passion that commands audience attention. To approach the microphone with just the right balance of terror and confidence may require a surge of adrenaline. Rather than block it, welcome it.

Making Friends with Fear

Before the adrenaline surge hits, ask yourself an important question: What am I really afraid of?

- Destroying my career? Nonsense, how can one speech ruin a career?
- Losing my job? I will get a better one.
- Not getting the contract or project? There are more of these at the other end of the telephone.
- Not getting the proposal passed? I will try again next month.
- Not being liked by my audience? Are they that important to me? Do I have to be liked or respected by them to like and respect myself?
- Triggering their anger? I can respect that energy and perhaps turn it around later. At least they care.
- Inspiring their pity? Ouch, this one hurts.

Hundreds of people who go through professional speech coaching have reported that the audience response they most fear is pity. Pity is the opposite of respect. It is the most debilitating response professionals can receive. Pity says, "You really made a fool of yourself up there and embarrassed both yourself and the organization. I feel sorry for you."

Once you confront your greatest fear, you can desensitize yourself to it. You can tell yourself:

- As long as I have my life, I make valuable contributions to my world.
- Negative responses offer me challenges and opportunities.
- Other people's reactions to me are their business with themselves—not mine. I may strive for acceptance, approval, and positive response, but I am not solely responsible for creating those reactions in each and every person.
- No matter what happens here today, I will survive.

Years ago, *Field and Stream* magazine did a playful review of D. H. Lawrence's book *Lady Chatterly's Lover*, a sexually provocative novel about an affair between the lady of the house and the resident gamekeeper. The reviewer found the book adequate on the science of gamekeeping but afflicted with too much extraneous material. For you to focus on fear and distress is like the reviewer missing the point of the "good parts."

How Do I Command Instant Credibility?

Suppose you are 22 years old, a recent graduate in engineering, and you are invited to talk to your department at work about highlights of your favorite college course, "Catastrophic Failures." You recognize that the other engineers will be skeptical about your background, and you would like to gain their respect. How can you command almost instant credibility?

Use three steps: Define your stance, include respected sources, and speak with confidence. In this example you might select the *novice* stance—refer to the textbook and professor for your course and include references to recent publications in engineering. Here is a possible opening:

Mark Twain's Cat and What We Learn from Catastrophic Failures

Mark Twain had a warning about experience: "We should be careful to get out of an experience only the wisdom that is in it—and stop there; lest we be like the cat that sits down on a hot stove-lid; she will never sit down on a hot stove lid again—and that is well; but also she will never sit down on a cold one anymore." In my recent course at M.I.T. on catastrophic failures, we focused on how to learn the right lessons from experience. Using the famous text by Reed and Gollens, Dr. Rita Gibbons conducted the symposium whose highlights I would like to give you this afternoon. So what I will cover today is not based on my own experience, which you know is limited, but on my studies with these authorities in our field.

Such an opening tends to disarm their skepticism and helps the audience listen more effectively. Use a similar strategy if you feel the audience may be skeptical because you are young, female, short, heavy, foreign, or otherwise "different" from them. Maryland Democrat Barbara Mikulski makes a point of her diminutive height. Going from stop to stop in her campaign for the Senate, she had an aide dramatically set a silver suitcase on its side behind the lectern. She stepped up, smiled, and said, "I'm the only Senatorial candidate to carry my own soapbox." She used the direct approach to counteract some people's tendency to dismiss her because she is short.

Prestigious publications yield excellent quotes for increasing your credibility. Consider the impact of these openings:

> *Dun's Business Month* reports that more than 75 percent of top executives serve as volunteers within 6 months of retirement.
>
> The *Journal of Applied Psychology* has news for us about advertising copy. Reverse type—light type on a dark background—slows reading almost 11 percent. Type set in all capital letters slows reading by more than 13 percent.
>
> The *Small Business Report* recently listed four compelling findings linking productivity and employee participation.
>
> *Nonprofit Piggy Goes to Market* reveals how the Children's Museum of Denver earns over $600,000 annually by running the museum as if it were a business.

These command attention by citing a prestigious source and by using specific facts or figures. Build your own credibility in the same way.

More Specific Tips

Until you adapt to the regular and natural adrenaline surge you feel, you may be lured by several unproductive temptations. Do not ingest alcohol, hot or cold drinks, or a large meal shortly before speaking. Alcohol, a depressant, may seem to relax you. But, of course, it slows your thinking and response time. Also, your heightened adrenaline state allows you to drink more alcohol before you begin to feel its impact. And then it may be too late. Hot or cold drinks affect your throat and vocal cords. Neither is relaxing or soothing. In addition, excess caffeine may overstimulate you. A large meal may soothe a nervous stomach, but it begs you to go to sleep for digestion. This is hardly the best way to keep the audience awake.

Instead, before you go on, disappear somewhere, perhaps into a restroom or closet, for a huge yawn or two. A good, healthy, full-bodied, and groaning yawn will do wonders for your poise. It relaxes the throat, opens the lungs, soothes the stomach, and stretches the muscles.

Yawning is an easy three-step skill.

1. Open your mouth as widely as possible.

2. Pull in three quick gasps of air.

3. Stretch your arms above your head and make any sounds and moves that feel natural.

Several yawns and a gentle roll of your neck around in a circle will help enormously. If no restroom or hallway is handy, try an empty office, a closet, or the back of the auditorium.

Sip room-temperature juice or water if you are thirsty. If your mouth dries up as you speak, give the audience a provocative question to think about for 10 seconds while you let your tongue relax fully into the bottom of your mouth. This natural reservoir has all the water you will ever need. You may also sip room-temperature water at the lectern.

Perhaps you saw a recent gadget catalog that featured a $119 item described as "Europe's Newest Thrill Machine." This item promised the ride of your life, bounding over obstacles in the world's newest sport. Only the photograph helped you realize that this exotic item was a pogo stick. The world today promises an amazing array of gadgets, gimmicks, and magic tricks. But a good old natural yawn and some room-temperature water can be much more effective for a public speaker.

Your Gray-Cell Theater

Mental rehearsal lets a speaker prepare in the theater of his or her own mind. Olympic swimmers are sometimes trained to think of their fingers as 6 inches longer than they are. They then imagine themselves stroking through the water with these extraordinarily long fingers. It helps. The swimmers report better focus and concentration on the strength and power in their hands. Their performance improves.

You can rehearse mentally for a presentation. Relax yourself physically. Create a picture in your mind of the coming event. See yourself being introduced. Stand to speak. Deliver your ideas with dynamic, yet disciplined power. Close with a call to action. Pause briefly to acknowledge the applause, and return to your seat. Create this picture with vivid details. What are you wearing, what food smells are still in the room, how loud is the microphone, and what do some of the individual faces in the audience look like? What, exactly, are you saying? Some presenters make a practice audiotape of the text of their speech, create this relaxed theater in their minds, and listen to the tape with their eyes closed as part of their rehearsal.

In over 18 years of research on peak performance, psychologist Charles Garfield found that the most unexpected quality of high performers in business and in sports was this use of mental rehearsal. Top producers prepare themselves thoroughly for challenges by mentally seeing themselves succeed in the situation before it happens.

Find Gold Rings instead of Bottlecaps

Overall, the best way to develop your own best natural style is to collect models of excellence in action, then to adapt and blend such elements as are appropriate to you.

Picture this scene: You are walking along a beach with a collecting sack and a metal detector. This is a very sophisticated device, one that has been programmed to accept your commands about what you want to discover. You can set this selector on bottlecaps, for example, and it will detect all the bottlecaps and pop-tops along the beach. You will have the joys of lots of noise on the machine and lots of bottlecaps in your sack. On the other end of the scale, you can set it on gold rings, and it will respond to only those. You get less noise, a lot less stuff in your sack, but what *is* there is worth something.

You have such a detector. You turn it on every day. And usually you keep it set on bottlecaps. You go around collecting this person's errors, that person's clumsy style, another person's odd expressions, still another's enormous capacity to bore everyone thoroughly. And when you go to review your treasures, you find only trash.

Why not set your detector on gold rings instead of bottlecaps? Why not collect one person's intent eye contact, another's compelling voice, and still another's gift of language which is like thought passing through a prism and emerging into a rainbow array of creative possibilities? Start to notice the smallest qualities that create excellence. How did that speaker weave in humor so appropriately? How did this one unify so many timely and diverse threads in an instantly recognizable design? How did the last speaker manage to finish exactly on time, having covered all the major points on the outline in 10 minutes less than the program indicated?

Gold rings are everywhere. If you empty all the trash out of your sack and start collecting gold rings, you will have handy models to help you set goals and extend your own excellence. These models will help you create your personal vision of yourself as an excellent speaker. They will offer you a range of effective options from which to build a style perfectly comfortable and natural for you. They will help make you a star in your own gray-cell theater—and the world at large!

Be Ready for Anything

After all your research and efforts, count on a few surprises. What do you do when the fire alarm clangs? Do you apologize after a huge blunder or even after a minor fluff? What do you say when you are a last-minute substitute for the vice-president? Naturally you will learn from experience in handling these and other issues. In the meantime, though, here are a few general guidelines for finetuning your skills.

The guidelines are simple: Stay calm, determine what can be done and by whom, select the most productive available alternative, do the best job possible under the circumstances, come through intact, and recycle whatever you learned about yourself, facilities, or audiences into preparation for the future.

Art Linkletter illustrates those guidelines in action in his story of a United Way fund drive in Detroit. Sitting next to Mr. and Mrs. Henry Ford on the platform during the picnic dinner, Linkletter noticed officials scurrying around the stage. He overheard someone say that the public address system was not working. The prospect of addressing 5000 people without such a system would certainly have made most speakers nervous. Not Linkletter. He continued chatting with Mrs. Ford on some other topic until she interrupted him to ask why he did not seem worried. "I'm concerned, but not worried," Linkletter commented.

"But what will you do?"

"I will go home."

"You will go home?" she repeated with alarm.

Art Linkletter calmly explained that he had nothing else to do. He knew nothing about the system and therefore could not fix it. It was impossible to speak without the system, and Mr. Ford was actively enlisting the support of people who could arrange an alternative. Rather than become embroiled in the crisis, Art Linkletter preserved his calm and his focus for the audience yet to be addressed—a mark of a real professional.

What About Emergencies?

There are very few absolutes in this book, but here is a serious one: Know how to handle yourself in a possible emergency. Once a fire alarm is clanging, it is too late. Train yourself to find out about the nearest fire exits from your meeting room. Resolve that in an emergency you will use your microphone and your role as leader to prevent panic and to stage an orderly and safe evacuation. If your meeting room is above the first floor, remind people not to use the elevators and tell them where the fire stairs are.

Never assume it is a false alarm. Sometimes it is not.

This advice may sound paranoid or morbid, but danger is one situation in which overreacting is better than underreacting. If you have not yet been confronted with this experience, your first reaction may be to play the sophisticated speaker ("We will get started up again when they can get the band to stop playing their one-note samba.") You and the microphone can help protect the lives of the people in that room. Pause a few seconds, if you like, to let your meeting planner or room monitor try to contact the office or the front desk on a house phone just in case it is a false alarm.

Prepare yourself mentally for this emergency, and you will never waste precious seconds asking yourself useless questions such as "Who is in charge here? What do I do now? How do we get out of here?" Your readiness can save lives.

A colleague once told about being awakened by a fire alarm in a huge international hotel at 5:30 A.M. She headed down the stairs to be turned back finally, with assurances that everything was under control. She smiled as she looked at her hands to realize that the only three things she brought with her were her room key, her passport, and her wedding ring.

Later that morning, as she addressed a group of 250 international attendees, the alarm sounded again. She told them the location of exits nearby and said, "You may stay or you may leave—but I am leaving." She unhooked her microphone and accompanied most of the group out of the room. On resuming the session after the all-clear notice, she told the story of the early morning evacuation and said, "If those three things were most precious to me this morning, I added to them in this room the possible responsibility for your lives. Let us hope the few minutes we lost from this session renew in us a sense of what we cherish most in our lives and in our work. Now let us get back to business."

The group clapped lustily—breaking their tension, subduing their fears, restoring their focus, preparing to work.

How to Recover from Fluffs or Fiascos

A *fluff* is a minor error that will go almost unnoticed if you ignore it. A *fiasco* is something giant and splendid in its awkwardness—something that will make a great story in a few years if only you survive the immediate cloud. Mistakes made while you are speaking seem dramatically

worse to you than to your audience. Remember that part of
this distortion is the standard "adrenaline magnification"
of being in the spotlight. Ignore small mistakes, minor mis-
pronunciations. Restate the idea correctly without apology,
and go on. Do not get embroiled in the emotional turmoil
of yelling at yourself ("I knew you would screw up, and
you did. You will never do anything right!"). Keep this
minor snag in perspective.

The giant and splendid fiasco does sometimes require
some comment—the more candid, honest, and disarming
the better. A sales representative was talking with the
board of directors of our professional group recently, and
he committed such a splendid fiasco. He raved about the
features of his product. He talked 3 minutes beyond the
time we had allowed him, and he was still going strong.
Our usually diligent timekeeper was letting him run on.
Several members looked at their watches. Someone started
ruffling notebook pages, and the speaker suddenly went
still.

He looked around at us with a stricken expression,
paused a moment, and said, "Damn, I have done it again."
His strong language and tone of voice caught us. "I can get
so wound up with this product and how well it can serve
your needs, I get carried away talking. Clearly you have
most of the data by now. Let me excuse myself and make
an appointment to meet for a few minutes tomorrow with
your executive committee and see what else is necessary
for a positive decision on this item. Thank you again for
your attention."

His candor and efficient exit kept him in the running
with an audience that was just starting to calcify against
him and his product.

Another potential fiasco occurs when you feel control of
the talk slipping away. You were on schedule in your outline, and suddenly you were mired down in an idea or
sentence that was leading nowhere. In ordinary conversa-

tion it is like telling the lead-in to a joke and remembering halfway through that you have forgotten the punch line. Again, candor and control keep the audience comfortably with you. It is better to stop, pause, say something, and restore focus. Trying to bluff your way through will usually lead you into further confusion and panic. Here are two variations on something to say:

- "It feels as if things are getting away from us a bit here. Let me review again the three key issues and our stance on this third one."
- "You may have heard it said that the race is not always to the swift nor the battle to the strong (pause . . .), but that is the way to bet. I would have bet that I could keep you with me on this swift, strong journey through ideas, but amazingly, I have confused even myself. Let us clarify the main point here."

What to Say If You Are Filling In for Someone Else

A "celebrity" speaker was invited and advertised, and you are a last-minute replacement. What do you say to the audience? Do you count on the fact that the apology made by your introducer will set the stage for you? No. Remember the frame of mind of the audience. Recognize that they may feel disappointed, cheated, or angry because they had hoped to have personal contact with your boss, the president, or some other industry celebrity. Remember the tension generated by such emotions, and revise the planned opening to help dissipate that tension. Add a 30- to 60-second transition before your opening. Here are three possible approaches, depending on the tone of the meeting:

1. What we thought was the light at the end of the tunnel turned out to be the headlamp of an oncoming train. So our president made an emergency trip back into the field to keep

*negotiations going. She promises to be available by tele-
phone from 6 until 10 tonight to any of you with compelling
concerns not covered in this address. So on to our topic . . . .*

*2. Yesterday's crisis in Cleveland demanded Bob's immedi-
ate presence. He asked me to deliver a personal message to
you before we go on to the speech: "I am sad to miss speaking
with you today. Your skills, energy, and loyalty have brought
us through some very tough times in the last 2 years, and I
wanted to thank you again in person and to share some directions for this coming year. When faced with the decision to
attend to the crisis or to speak with you, I realized you need
only one sentence from me: 'The crisis is past, and we are
triumphant.' As you hear these words, I am working to make
that message a reality. Listen now to the plans I am confident
we will need for that more profitable future." Here, now, is
Bob's address . . . .*

*3. I feel a little like Dolly Parton being asked to substitute
for Henry Kissinger. Although we are well respected in our
separate fields, I am not sure anyone will take me seriously.
Please think, though, for a moment of the things we have in
common—love of work, family, community, and country—
instead of thinking of our differences. Those common loyal-
ties might make it easier for you to hear what I have been
sent to say—and what I'm proud and honored to present.*

Once you have completed a graceful transition, deliver
the speech as the invited presenter would have done it. Of
course, you do not try to imitate the dynamics of delivery;
just be as true to the content as possible. If you are working
from a prepared text and have even half an hour of notice,
find a quiet corner or closet and read the entire text aloud
once. Memorize the opening and closing sentences, so you
can keep full eye contact during these critical moments.

At this point people sometimes complain, "But I cannot
in all conscience say these things. I do not agree with

them, and furthermore I am a career employee, not an executive who job-hops with each change in management or administration. I do not choose to be associated with these policies or approaches." If this is a true ethical dilemma, you may have to refuse to substitute (and consider whether you are working in the right place). More often, these are mental stall tactics to postpone accepting a responsibility you feel unprepared for. Move immediately past such barriers. Recognize that you may be the one talking, but you are primarily a conduit for ideas. Yours are not the views that the program advertised, and yours are not the words the audience came to hear. Deliver the promise. Substitute graciously by using a good opening transition and staying with the scheduled message.

Key Ideas

- The best blend of delivery techniques appropriate to your personality, your message, and your audience is your most successful style.
- Consider several effective ways to open with impact.
- Explore all five critical elements in presentation dynamics.
- Honor your time contract with the meeting planner and the audience.
- Use specific ideas to handle questions and answers with comfort and confidence.
- Learn to channel nervousness into presentation energy.
- Blend your "gold ring" samples into a model of speaking excellence in your own style.
- Rehearse mentally to practice and exercise that vision regularly.
- Be prepared for anything.

CHAPTER SEVEN

Mining Humor and Spice from The Wall Street Journal and Other Sources

The Risk Paradox

Imagine crossing 80 feet above a canyon on a zip wire. You climb to the launching point, strap in safely, step off the firm earth, zip screaming through the green forest for seconds vividly alive in time, and touch ground on the other side. The experience is thrilling and exhilarating precisely *because* it is risky.

So many people are afraid to use humor in presentations because it is too risky. They are afraid to try and fail. What if they get halfway across the canyon and the wire breaks? What is they get almost across and there is no firm ground on the other side? The paradox is that by not accepting the risk of using humor they face a greater risk—that of having audience's attention wander away, permanently.

Humor Redefined

Stop taking humor so seriously! Humor is more than just jokes and comedy. Recognize the wider range of humor.

See and hear it all around you. Some forms of humor fit comfortably into business presentations. But you help limber up your mind when you think of using even startling or unique facets of humor. Here are examples of types of humor:

Surprise

You open an important meeting by taking a stalk of broccoli from your briefcase and comparing your current project to the broccoli.

Exaggeration

When asked a concrete question, you reply with an even more concrete answer. For instance, you are asked, "In trying to sell an idea to a client, how do you know when to stop? How do you keep from beating a dead horse?" You reply, "I walk away when the horse even starts to look sick. With so many people around who could be good clients, why should I wear myself down on the tough ones?"

Incongruity

The entertainer juggles an apple, a chain saw (running), and a bowling ball, remarking, "You thought I would not be able to do this. You doubted. You thought I would not succeed because they are all different (pause) colors."

Verbal Play

The Wall Street Journal headline on Valentine's Day, 1985, read: "San Diego Zoo a Veritable Hot Bed of Activity." The article explained that the zoo had wanted to encourage some of its animals to have babies. Modern reproductive technology offered many alternatives, chemical and mechanical. Instead, the zoo installed heated waterbeds for selected animals. The beds encouraged amorous activity and raised the animal birthrate. You might use this anecdote to remind your listeners to check their own assumptions carefully—how often do we reach for the complex, technological solution when something more simple, more natural, perhaps even more pleasant is nearby?

Visual Play

On your way to a session on setting priorities you see a woman, roundly pregnant, carrying a globe of the world. You are quite taken with the idea that these double round objects signify life from the personal and global perspectives. This woman carries the future and the world with her today. You use this visual metaphor in your group to explore priorities based on the individual and on the whole organization.

Appropriateness

The title of the biography of Ray Kroc, founder of McDonald's fast-food chain, is *Grinding It Out*. Here is a snippet from an introduction of Lee Iacocca: "Mr. Iacocca must have known his destiny, even during his years at Ford. Look at his name. The letters stand for "I Am Chairman of the Chrysler Corporation of America."

Concreteness

It is 6 A.M. on a rainy morning in dark February. You are starting a 300-mile drive all alone to pick up an urgently needed part from a supplier. The first exit you pass on the

highway has a neon sign, bright against the morning glow,
perfectly appropriate to your morning. It's a Shell station
sign with the letter S burned out. In spite of it all, you
smile.

How Do I Spice Up a Hopelessly Dull Topic?

Business presentations are notoriously dull, but they need
not be. Just as you used resources and publications to build
your credibility, do not forget that those resources are also
helpful in building audience interest. One speaker was
recently challenged to help set the tone for his organization's strategic planning session. He wanted an opening
that helped people understand the challenge of trying to
project the changes they might face in the next 3, 5, 10, and
20 years. He wanted to reinforce the message that just because they were industry leaders today, they should not
become complacent. He also wanted to capture and hold
their attention without being too solemn or stuffy. Here is
his opening:

Risqué to Passé: Business Lessons from the Demise of the Playboy Clubs

June 23, 1986, a front-page article in The Wall Street Journal
*began, "On a frigid night in February 1960, the world's first
playboy club began its long run as the hottest spot in town.
The crowd was so large that hundreds were left in the street,
pleading with doorman Ray Lovelacy for a peek inside. [Just
one generation later,] their sons aren't impressed. There are*

*health clubs and singles bars where the women aren't inac-
cessible. The bunny costume no longer seems daring. Strip
joints are abundant and don't tax the imagination . . . .
Having helped to change mores, Playboy is now tamer than
the competition." There are three messages to us in this
story, and we'll spend the next 12 minutes considering them.*

This presentation closed with:

*Let us hope that when we are featured on the front page of
The Wall Street Journal 20 years from now, it will be to celebrate the success of some of the very plans, visions, and directions we define here today.*

Do not forget literature as a source of interesting material. A friend once made a collection of the first sentences
of all the classic books. This collection was a gold mine of
idea starters. Take, for example, the opening sentence of
Thornton Wilder's Pulitzer Prize winning novel. Here is
an opening based on that sentence:

Bridges to Understanding: The Bottom Line and the True Big Picture

*The community service project we initiate today reminds me
of the opening of Thornton Wilder's novel* The Bridge of San
Luis Rey: *"On Friday noon, July the twentieth, 1714, the
finest bridge in all Peru broke and precipitated five travellers
into the gulf below."*

The novel tells the story of Brother Juniper, a monk who witnesses the tragedy and then asks why. "Why did this happen to those five? . . . If there were any pattern in a human life, surely it could be discovered mysteriously latent in those lives so suddenly cut off."

Our purpose today is to start building a bridge that will not break—a bridge of literacy that will help adults build skills latent in their own lives, a bridge that will connect them to new opportunities.

The presentation concludes:

By the end of Wilder's book, Brother Juniper sensed a grand and spiritual design in the collapse of the bridge. He sensed a big picture too vast for his comprehending. Tonight we began a project which may seem similarly vast but which we nonetheless commit to. This is a bottom line and a big picture worthy of our efforts. Let us join together tonight to build that bridge.

And here are two more morsels you can experiment with turning into interesting openings and closings. Both are front-page briefs from the December 12, 1985, issue of *The Wall Street Journal:*

- *An ethnic restaurant in New York calls itself Curry in a Hurry.*
- *Buyers of the $95 book* How to Marry the Man of Your Choice *get their money back if they aren't engaged within four years.*

Benefits of Humor

Humor need not command waves of laughter. It may merely prompt the crack of a smile in the mind, to let an idea slip in and make itself at home. Walk around hungry and thirsty for humor, novelty, light thoughts, and interesting scenes. You will find them.

Humor refocuses audience attention, it brings attention back to the speaker. Picture yourself as a member of an audience as you listen to a presenter. Your mind floats back to thinking of that prospect you intend to call tomorrow morning. You begin to script the conversation. Suddenly the room around you erupts into laughter. You turn away from your private planning party back to the meeting at hand. You wonder what you missed, but the laugh reminded you to listen.

Humor reinforces ideas and implants those ideas more firmly in the audience's memory.

Let us suppose you are a guest speaker at a strategic planning conference for executives in your industry. As keynote presenter, you wish to challenge them to go beyond traditional solutions. You want them to become as innovative as possible. You want them to see that creativity has an important and legitimate role in business today.

You say to them, "How many of you have ever purchased retroactive auto insurance? First you have the accident. Then you buy the insurance." (They smile.) "Well, how many have had any form of retroactive insurance? None? Consider this report from the front page of The Wall Street Journal, *February 11, 1981: 'The MGM Grand secured 170 million dollars in retroactive fire insurance to cover claims in last year's tragic fire at the Las Vegas casino.' "*

Imagine the meeting where this idea emerged. Executives were sitting around with their heads in their hands worrying, "What are we going to do?" as tendrils of smoke curled out of the ashes. Suddenly someone says, "Let us buy some insurance." What do you think the others at that meeting thought, felt, said? That we will never know. What we do know is the result: The MGM Grand stunned the business world by its innovative purchase of retroactive fire insurance.

"Well, colleagues, we are here today to consider our own industry. I challenge you to realize that creativity is alive and well and living on Wall Street, in healthy businesses, and in this session here today. Anytime today you see the glow of an idea, a lightbulb, a candle, a cigarette, remember retroactive fire insurance. Someone had to think of it before it could happen. As we discuss and deliberate, keep asking yourself if there is any retroactive fire insurance out there we should be creating. Let us get to work."

Rather than just telling the group to be creative, you have reinforced that idea. Your group is likely to think about it several times today and perhaps tell someone about it tomorrow.

Another benefit of humor is that it prevents information overload. It keeps you from dumping too much data on poor, unsuspecting ears.

One hallmark of the maturing speaker is to stop asking, "How can I cover the greatest amount of material?" and start asking, "How can I cover a few essential points and move my listeners to action?" Humor helps here. It gives the audience a breather, a chance to absorb what they are hearing.

Humor eases tension. Notice the emotional shift in a meeting or session when someone asks a hostile question or challenges an idea or fact. Suddenly the air sharpens with suspense. Can the speaker handle it? Will there be a fight? What will happen next?

If a speaker responds with equal hostility, the audience often sides with the questioner. After all, if the speaker attacks this person, is anyone safe from similar attack? If the speaker responds defensively, some audience members remain loyal, if grudgingly sympathetic. Others wonder what there is to be defensive about and side with the questioner. If the speaker responds with humor, though, the audience usually stays in focus and feels they are in good hands.

Al Capp, creator of the "Li'L Abner" comic strip, toured college campuses with patriotic speeches during the Vietnam war. A demonstrator in one session interrupted Capp by shouting obscenities. Tension bristled. Capp paused, looked directly at the student, and calmly remarked, "You've given us your name, sir. Now do you have a question?" A wave of laughter and relief rolled through the hall. The demonstrator left, his power to disrupt punctured by humor.

Johnny Carson sometimes reminds us that he knows he is in for a tough night when he looks down to see a kindly, red-haired grandmother from Indiana in the front row with the slogan "Born to Heckle" tattooed on her arm.

Suppose you were given the task of defining your company's market position by inventing a slogan that says exactly what you do. Weeks go by, and still you do not have that perfect slogan. Now, someone at a staff meeting challenges you for taking so long. Suppose you answer your challenger, "This slogan is so vitally important to the marketing of our lines in the next 10 years that I refuse to be rushed. After all, would you like to be the person who rushed this slogan through before testing it on his car-repair clients: Why go elsewhere to be cheated? We can do it for you here."

And finally, humor is healthy! Laughter is good for your body. A lighthearted attitude helps reduce stress and tension, both major contributors to many illnesses. Art Gliner, whose business card reads "Head Joker, The Humor Communication Company," developed a program called the "Humor Approach to Excellence." This program helps business people channel their play spirit into fun, creativity, and eventually, productivity. Business America is lightening up!

Humor Guidelines

The humor guidelines are simple. If you have material that you can use comfortably which yields one or more of the above benefits, use it. Your humor can refocus audience attention, reinforce key ideas, prevent information overload, ease tension, or allow for healthy laughter. If it does some of those things, feel free to use it. If it does none of those things, why waste the time?

What to Avoid

Stay away from ethnic or sexist stories and any others that are in questionable taste. Think of every joke you tell as having your name on it forever after. Never underestimate the conservative nature of your audience. You are there to promote some idea, product, or service. You are there to practice magnetic marketing, to attract people. Why take a chance on offending them when it is not necessary? When in doubt, leave it out.

Getting Comfortable

Stop a moment, and do an exercise on a separate sheet of paper. Write your name three times. Now write your name three times with the opposite hand. Could you do it at all? Probably. And did you observe that it was clumsy, awkward? Was everything big and exaggerated?

That is exactly how you learned most skills. The more often you practice something, the better you get at it. If you ever broke your writing arm as a youth and had to write with the "other" hand for many weeks, you got much better over time. Give yourself the same permission to be clumsy at first in using humor.

When you find a story, quote, or article that illustrates a key idea, work on it. Develop the 1-minute version stripped of details. Work that into a longer story with descriptions and drama. Practice both of them 5, 10, 50 times. Try them on lunch companions, colleagues, family, strangers on a train. Play with the timing, the details, the punch line. Then use them in your presentations and reshape them based on audience responses. You get comfortable with humor through practice. You know your stories so well that you never have to apologize halfway through because you forgot the punch line.

Best Sources of Material

By far the best humor comes from real life. We talk more about this in a moment. First, let us answer questions about other sources.

Why look for humor in *The Wall Street Journal?* It is a powerful source of humor because most people do not expect it to be funny. They are surprised and delighted to hear something entertaining from this staid and respected publication. Why do we fail to realize that the *Wall Street Journal* is in business to sell papers and a little humor helps them sell?

You therefore capitalize on the inherent novelty of the article or idea and on its respected source at the same time, to increase the effect. *The Wall Street Journal* is also lodged in the minds of most listeners as "something I should start reading regularly." When you bring them condensed and focused nuggets from *The Wall Street Journal,* you are calming their guilt and making them feel more professional.

Of course, any publication will have periodic splashes of humor. Do not expect to find something every day, and do not wait for screamingly funny articles. Look for things that are intriguing. Look for tidbits you can shape into something humorous. Take this item from *The Wall Street Journal,* front page of the June 27, 1985, issue:

Ocean Spray Cranberries, Inc. gives fortune cookies to employees to mark its arrival on the Fortune 500 list of big companies. The message: "A tasteful thanks."

What would Joan Rivers do with that information? What would Bill Cosby, Tom Peters, or Mark Russell do? Think of other events a company could mark, and come up with appropriate souvenirs for these events:

• When we get into the black

- When we get written up positively in a major magazine
- When we get named "company of the year"
- When we get listed in Fortune 8000
- When we make it through the week
- When we declare bankruptcy

Play with these ideas. Invite others to join in your play. See things as funny, say things as funny. People will smile.

What are other good sources of humor? Do not overlook the obvious. Good comedy services offer subscribers timely humor on a regular basis. The best is Current Comedy, established by Bob Orben, a highly respected comedy writer with a prolific output. Orben has also published a wealth of humor books. Contact Current Comedy at 700 Orange Street, Wilmington, DE, 19801, or call (302) 656-2209 for further information about humor material available.

Your library also has books on humor and famous quotes. Also try *Reader's Digest* anthologies. What you get from any of these sources is only the beginning of your material. It is how you shape and deliver it that counts.

Now, What about True Stories?

These stories are sometimes the hardest to develop objectively because they happened to you. Look back on the triumphs and blunders of your life. What are the stories you tell at reunions and New Year's Eve parties? These stories are easy to remember because they really happened. They are chunks from your life—nobody else can rightly claim them. Here are a few tips for using such stories:

Relevance

Make sure the story is relevant to a key idea or point you are making. Shave and shape the story specifically to highlight that key point. Draw the relationship clearly after you tell the story.

Be Human

Make yourself human. Do not be the all-knowing, all-competent hero—you can certainly save the day in the end, but only after some chagrin or embarrassment. Do not be a complete boob either. The story should end with your winning respect again.

Avoid Cuteness

Avoid endearing language and baby talk. Do not refer to "my wifey" or "my hubby."

Roots in Reality

You sometimes exaggerate for dramatic effect in a story, but keep the roots in reality or you may forget the ending!

Here is an example of a true story used to illustrate one concept of magnetic marketing—that anything and everything you do can help build or hamper business.

Jack Weinhart, Vice-president of Pleasant Hawaiian Holidays, tells the story of how he once made a sales call on the president of the newly formed NFL franchise football team, the Dallas Cowboys. Weinhart was then vice-president of Braniff and intended to interest this gentleman in signing a contract for team travel and fan-group charters. As Weinhart entered the office, the man greeted him warmly and said, "Before we talk, let me show you two letters." Weinhart read the first letter, which was an appeal to Dallas businesses to buy season tickets to support this raw and undeveloped football team. This early loyalty would ensure these supporters, the letter said, choice seats in the future when the team's success would create great demands for such tickets. The second letter contained the same text with a handwritten response across the bottom: "Not interested in season tickets!" This scrawl was signed by the president of Braniff.

After Weinhart finished reading the second letter, the gentleman beamed at him and said, "Well, Jack, what was it you wanted today?" Weinhart's instant reply? "Why, six season tickets, of course!" This is a great story Weinhart can now use to help people at all levels of an organization recognize that everything they do can affect the success of the company.

How Do I Keep Track of Good Material?

Once you start to be alert for interesting idea starters, you have to develop a system to keep them accessible. Such a system can range from a simple clipping file to a computerized cross-referenced collection. Use whatever matches your needs and your temperament.

Secretary of Transportation Elizabeth Dole keeps a special humor file. "A lot of humor I pick up even in church . . . . My minister is very good with humor, and I jot down notes as I go along. When I hear a good speech, I make notes and drop them into my humor file. When I'm going to a particular group and I want to pull up something that might be relevant to them, I'll look through what I've collected . . . to see if there is something appropriate to this group."

The organizing pattern most often used in books of quotations or anecdotes is to alphabetize entries by topics. That might work for you, too. Some people prefer to keep items in a big box or notebook and leaf through occasionally. I clip and collect everything that intrigues me at all and put it in one place in my office. About once a month I review the stack. If an item does not hold up to a second reading, it probably will not grab an audience either. If it is still interesting, it goes into my current three-ring binder. About every 2 years I start a new binder.

Whatever your system, do yourself a favor and write the source and date on the clippings. This gives you the confidence to quote and attribute the material accurately.

What Are Some Good Collections of Quotes?

No matter what your system for filing ideas, you will do well to have a resource library of quotes available. Here are three personal favorites:

- *2,715 One-Line Quotations for Speakers, Writers, and Raconteurs,* by Edward F. Murphy, Crown Publishing, New York, 1981. Most of the quotations are shorter than the title but just as descriptive and valuable.
- *2,100 Laughs for All Occasions,* by Robert Orben, Doubleday, New York, 1983. This is one of Orben's 46 books on topical and timely humor on issues from football to social security. A former professional TV comedy writer, Presidential speech writer, and prolific author, Orben's topical material provides the nucleus for timely and humorous material of your own. Watch for his most current works.
- *Peter's Quotations: Ideas for Our Times,* by Dr. Lawrence J. Peter, Bantam, New York, 1977. This is a classic of pithy sayings. From Socrates to Woody Allen, this collection includes gems of brevity, wisdom, and wit from the author of the bestselling book *The Peter Principle.*

Why Do People Recommend Toastmasters International?

Toastmasters International is a nonprofit organization of more than 4000 clubs located in over 40 countries. Dr. Ralph C. Smedley established Toastmasters in 1924 in Santa Ana, California, to help people learn to speak more effectively. Membership is open to anyone over age 18, and dues are nominal. Upon joining a club in your community, you receive the *Toastmasters Communication and Leadership Program Manual.* The manual contains a series of 15 speech assignments designed to provide instruction and practice in the basic techniques of public speaking. You progress through the manual at your own pace and receive valuable feedback from trained observers throughout your participation. You also become a trained observer and are better able to coach yourself and others through the skills you develop in Toastmasters.

For professionals with the time and predictable schedule to devote to Toastmasters, this is an excellent learning opportunity. For more information, write Toastmasters International, P.O. Box 10400, Santa Ana, CA 92711, (714) 542-6793.

If, however, you decide that you need a "quick-fix" for a critical presentation coming up soon, consider a course or individual coaching. Quality in such programs varies greatly. Be sure to ask some important questions:

• Will the course include videotaping?

• How long will each participant actually have on tape?

• How many students per coach are in the course?

• Do you get to keep your tape?

• Will tapings be of previously selected material, or will you customize your own?

- Is there follow-up available before the next major presentation?
- Who else will be in the session? Might I compromise my company or my position?
- What are the credentials of the presenter-coach?

These questions help you decide among the sessions which promise to explore 200 strategies for 100 people in only 4 hours for a mere $95 and those which charge $10,000 for 1 day of private, customized coaching. Most professionals need something in between.

Solving Two Common Humor Dilemmas

Dilemma 1

You tell a story, and the audience does not laugh. Solution? Stop worrying. Even show business professionals take time to warm up their groups. Many send out preprogram comedy acts to be sure this audience is capable of laughter. When you do not get the response you are hoping for, do not panic. Say to yourself, "They are laughing inside, and it will come out later as hiccoughs!" Here are two recovery lines used by professionals in the right setting:

1. "What are you, an audience or an oil painting?"

2. "So what is this, a staring ovation?"

Try these sometime in a low-risk setting (one where you will not get fired), and see how you feel and how the audience reacts. Do not feel defeated and give up, though, if they do not laugh right away. Keep trying. Remember the handwriting exercise. Give yourself plenty of time to be clumsy so later you will be enormously graceful.

Dilemma 2

You heard a great joke on television last night. You planned to use it, and two speakers in front of you have already used it. Solution? Do not use it. *Or* tell the group you are going to lead them in choral recitation. Say the first sentence of the joke, close your mouth, and conduct them while retelling the rest—move your arms grandly like an orchestra conductor. *Or* tell them you wanted to tell the joke but you were shocked and crestfallen that a fellow professional would crassly steal material from you that you had stolen just last night.

Humor is one of the most powerful skills in the speaker's array. Collect humor, practice using it, and reap the rewards.

Laugh Your Way to the Top

One final note on humor. Humor is healthy for your career. Robert Half International, a financial executive, accounting, and data processing recruiter, recently commissioned a study to examine corporate attitudes toward employees with a sense of humor. Burke Marketing Research, Inc., interviewed personnel directors and vice-presidents of 100 of America's 1000 largest companies. An overwhelming 84 percent responded that employees with a sense of humor do a better job than those lacking that quality. Moreover, 32 percent also felt that the people in top management had the best sense of humor. This compares to 28 percent for middle managers and 18 percent for other staff personnel.

"People with a sense of humor," Robert Half commented, "tend to be more creative, less rigid, and more willing to consider and embrace new ideas and methods.

In today's business environment, if you haven't got a good sense of humor, the joke could be on you."

Training yourself to locate, practice, polish, and use humor not only will improve your overall humor IQ, but also will let others see that you are the material of which executive leaders are made. What a fine, healthy prescription for success!

Key Ideas

- The risk of not using humor can be greater than the risk of using it.
- Select items appropriate to your style from the seven forms of humor.
- Appreciate the five benefits that humor offers.
- Guidelines help you decide what to select and what to avoid.
- Identify good sources of material in addition to your true stories.
- Humor is healthy for your career.

CHAPTER EIGHT

Lights, Camera, Terror

Why Are Video Skills Important?

Probably the single biggest emerging challenge to business communicators today is that they will need on-camera skills within their careers. Video annual reports, video pamphlets, video product demonstrations, video training sessions for employees, cable and broadcast interview opportunities, video-enhanced speaking at conferences—it is everywhere. Sooner or later, it affects us all. Consider these illustrations.

The Direct Marketing Association awarded its 1985 prize for the most innovative use of direct-mail techniques to Robert O'Keefe, who marketed his product—younger brother Jim O'Keefe—to college football coaches. Robert mailed resumes and videotapes of Jim in action on the field. The $300 investment yielded a full $15,000 scholarship to Boston University.

Most of us would think that having a negative interview with Mike Wallace on *60 Minutes* would be emotionally draining and economically damaging. Not so, say three North Texas State University finance professors. These professors tracked the stock prices of 13 companies that were featured on the CBS show in the past 5 years. Their initial assumption, according to Associate Professor Wallace Davidson, was "that if Mike Wallace rakes you over the coals, your stock would go down."

Surprisingly, the shares of the 13 companies did 12 percent better on average than the rest of the stock market for 15 days after the show aired, even though only one of the firms had been portrayed favorably.

Years ago a rising professional predicted, "I think there is a world market for about five computers." Thomas J. Watson, who made that prediction, later became chairman of IBM. Watson's perception of the role of technology changed. So also will ours as we become increasingly skilled and dependent on the video channels of business communication.

Public speaking skills will always be critical, so do not ignore them. But think video also.

Marshall McLuhan commented, "We don't know who discovered water, but we can be pretty sure it was not a fish." He reminds us that we have lived in a world full of television for so long that we are not necessarily alert to its impact on business communication. The *Wall Street Journal* reports that Hughes Aircraft recently selected four engineers from among 600 applicants for participation in a space shuttle project. They had four selection criteria: good technical skills, high level of maturity, strong corporate record, and the ability to deal with the media.

Had these applicants selected engineering as a field years ago because they wanted to go on television one day? No! Most likely they were attracted to the logic, the order, the pattern, and the predictability of science. They selected a field in which they could prosper through logical skills rather than through communication or people skills.

Yet what do they find, as they seek one of the most prestigious and challenging positions available in their industry? Suddenly they need the ability to speak to the media, to represent their organization powerfully in public. Although you may initially scoff at the idea of facing the camera yourself, start being aware of the increasing role of video and television in the business communication environment.

Hughes Aircraft is only one of many organizations recognizing the need for today's professionals to have television skills. Many business presentations could be done through video, television, or teleconference. Now we discuss a few specifics.

Both political parties used video-enhanced speeches at their last conventions. Anyone planning to present in any convention center, large auditorium, or major ballroom should be prepared for the day they tell you that you will be simulcast. Yes, 16 feet of face will be projected onto one or more screens behind you simultaneously as you speak. Your every smile, frown, grimace, glance at your notes, gesture, and bead of perspiration dance large for all to see. Are you ready for the sight of your teeth 12 inches tall and your eyebrows doing aerobics in public?

Today only a handful of companies produce a video annual report. They select this format, though, because such a report communicates vividly to shareholders the living, producing, dynamic nature of the operation. Stockholders see and hear the people, the equipment, the products that constitute the company. How soon might you be involved in this powerful format?

Your industry calls for proposals to present information, not a sales pitch, over a massive international teleconference. You realize that you could do a valuable session on "What to Look for When You Decide to Invest in (Your Field)." The session is intended to reach 30,000 people worldwide. Are you ready to volunteer?

You have a new product line to introduce to your sales teams across the country and around the world. You also have an orientation program to conduct monthly at scattered sites. In both cases you want to ensure that everyone receives exactly the same, complete, accurate information. Video lets you guarantee the uniformity of such a presentation. You can also prepare intensively for one high-impact program to be used repeatedly in new audiences without growing stale.

Because you prepare this tape only once, you can afford to use your most productive and dynamic presenters. Whether the playback sessions are conducted in Diamond Lake, Oregon, or Budapest, Hungary, all participants will receive the same basic information. Are you involved yet in producing such custom-tailored video for your organization? Should you be?

In a world of video dating services and video therapist selection, does it surprise you to know that there are also video resumes? One company, InterVIEW, provides video services for executives wishing more personal impact than a printed form allows. Paul Beaudry, the firm's president, rehearses the job candidate in a few basic camera skills and then tapes some responses to standard interview questions. Such video resumes can be a powerful preliminary screening tool. They save travel time and money, allowing you to go anywhere on film overnight. Could you convince a faraway potential employer or client of your skills via video?

Who would have thought that 1984 would see one of the world's most respected traditions in great peril? Yes, 1984 was the year someone tampered with Girl Scout cookies. Suddenly, Girl Scouts and their leaders were called upon to inform the public and restore confidence in the product. Obviously, we never know ahead of time the source or nature of the next crisis, tampering, hijacking, accident, or scandal. Ask yourself, "Could I speak out effectively for my industry in an emergency?"

Your company is approaching its 25th anniversary and you realize that all the historic photographs could blend with interviews of some pioneers in the company. This would make a priceless archive document. Could you plan and participate in such a video?

The local news media regularly question the social conscience of your company. You are invited to give a 1-minute reply on the "Speak Out" segment. Could you present a concerned, persuasive snapshot of the benefits your company brings to the community?

This series of glimpses illustrates that video is versatile and increasingly universal—from astronaut training to Sunday school to police work to sales programs to speech training. It is everywhere and growing. Why fight it? You and television share a destiny.

Are Video Skills Difficult to Learn?

No. There are three main snags to be aware of: video shock, the Walter Cronkite complex, and the slippery plateau.

Video Shock

Video shock is the normal response people have to seeing and hearing themselves the first few times on video. Remember that automatic reaction you had the first time you heard your voice on a tape recorder? "That is not me," you appealed; but other people assured you that it was. Triple that shock, and you can estimate your reaction to your image on television.

Think for a moment. You are used to seeing yourself in still photographs or barely moving in a mirror as you comb your hair. But on video, suddenly your eyebrows seem to be doing push-ups. Your mouth moves so much. You face is not at all symmetric. Surely you are younger and thinner than that. Surely you have more hair. Surely this cannot be accurate; it must be the lighting.

The solution for video shock is to tape yourself in private and watch 10 to 20 minutes of yourself in several different tapings before you begin to objectively assess areas for change or development. This could be done in a conference room at the office or in your den with borrowed or rented equipment. Once you have watched yourself several times, you can separate yourself and your discomfort from that face and voice and ask objectively, "What am I doing well that comes across powerfully? What might I change to get more or better results?"

The Walter Cronkite Complex

Every day on television we see the video descendants of Walter Cronkite. These professionals have cool polish and natural ease, yet a committed, even emotional way of presenting their material. We sit back in awe at what appears to be raw, natural talent.

Were these people always so polished? No, they learned their craft just as you learned yours. Most admit to having experienced emotions ranging from butterflies to stone-cold panic. They got good the same way you will. They observed and studied excellence in others. They practiced, reviewed, adapted, practiced, reviewed, adapted. They still keep this cycle going. Free yourself from the misleading myth that you will never get good at this if it does not come automatically.

Replace that myth with the conviction that you will develop these skills gradually until you get the results you want. Bury your Walter Cronkite complex, and get on with the challenge of being a versatile communicator.

The Slippery Plateau

And now to the third deterrent. We know that a plateau is supposed to be flat and firm. It is a place where, after a long climb, you can pause and rest. This particular plateau is

described as slippery to remind you that once you get accustomed to one level of video challenges, technology will
spawn new ones. There is no permanent resting plateau.
Once you master one type of microphone, new ones come
along. Why not someday a microphone that fits unobtrusively behind your front teeth?

The slippery plateau of ever-changing technology is a
problem that can work to our advantage. It keeps us alert to
the world around us and encourages us to adapt.

How You Look on Camera

The audience responds to your message at many levels.
When they see your frantically darting eyes or wringing
hands, they do not usually think, "My, look at that talented
professional who is nervous." Instead they think, "Why is
that person so jumpy?" How you look on camera helps the
audience decide whether to believe and act on what you
are saying. Comfort and confidence about how you look
help you focus on your message instead of worrying about
your mannerisms.

You Do Not Control Everything

How you look on camera is not entirely up to you. Lighting, camera angles, the variety of shots the director selects—all these factors have great impact on how you come
across. Rarely, however, do you have anything to say about
these factors. If invited, you may want to see yourself on a
monitor, request a certain placement of lights or specific
shooting angles, or ask to be filmed in a setting reflecting
your work. Ordinarily, however, trust the professionals,
and do not worry about technical details.

Making Friends with Your Face

As mentioned briefly in an example in Chapter 5, your face
is your most important television visual aid. Do not worry
that you think it is overly expressive. Do not worry that
your nose or teeth or eyes are not perfectly formed. There
are very few symmetric faces in the world. Picture Katharine Hepburn, Albert Einstein, Joe Namath—interesting faces, expressive faces, not symmetric faces.

As mentioned in Chapter 5, you may want to accept or
request makeup. Fran Campbell, a specialist in this area,
reports that both men and women can enjoy three benefits
from television makeup: First, as the lights and camera
tend to flatten your features, makeup restores some of your
natural dimensions. Second, makeup helps you look
healthy, vital, and alert which encourages viewers to be
more attentive. Third, a light dusting of translucent powder reduces the glare and reflection caused by studio
lights. It also helps hide sweat which may be caused by the
lights or by your feelings. Powder helps you counter the
nervous, sweaty look with one of relaxed assurance.

If makeup is not offered, take care of it yourself. Women
usually use their regular makeup with slight dramatic emphasis. You do not need the drama of stage makeup—just a
hint beyond the everyday. Both men and women may want
to have baby powder or corn starch and a large, soft brush
for applying powder lightly. If you are under the lights for
long, check your "shine" level on each break. You can
freely apply many layers of translucent powder before it
shows.

Your hair is another challenge in learning to love your
face. Wear a style natural for you, but one that leaves most
of your face visible. Two problems can arise if you have
lots of hair or no hair.

If you have lots of hair on top, remember that some lights
shine down on you from above. If your hair is high and full,

it may cast a shadow over your whole face. If you have long bangs down over your eyebrows, you similarly rob the viewer of a significant portion of your face and its messages. Consider arranging your hair so that it does not detract from your face.

If you have no hair on top, remember that your scalp, like your face, may reflect studio lights and begin to perspire. A light spray of a powdered deodorant may help, or you can apply the same powder you use on your face.

Clothes that Cooperate

As emphasized earlier, select clothes that cooperate—ones that underline your message, not argue with it. High society divorcee Roxanne Pulitzer appeared on the Phil Donohue Show in very casual clothing, proceeded to assume gymnastic seating positions as she was interviewed, spoke openly about her photo spread in *Playboy* magazine, and complained that the courts had given her husband custody of their young sons. Yes, she said, she had dressed exactly this way and spoken this way in court during the custody hearings. The audience respected her contention that her clothing and manner did not reflect her ability as a mother. Some, however, suggested that if she cared enough about wanting custody, she might have played down her freedom of expression in order to gain a different goal.

People listen to and react to what you wear and how you act as well as to what you say. Whether this is an artificial or hypocritical standard is not the issue. The issue is that people judge and respond to what they see. Appropriate clothes on video are those that support, or at least do not distract from, your message. Here are additional details on the basic suggestions covered in Chapter 5.

Avoid

- Stark white, red, or black in large quantity because these colors bloom, bleed, or fade away on camera
- Large, bold, high-contrast designs or prints, which scream for attention, upstaging your ideas
- Large metallic decorations or jewelry which reflect lights and can even create noise
- Narrow, repeating stripes, such as herringbone, which wave and weave on camera

Choose

- Subdued or neutral colors appropriate to your style and coloring
- Clothing with a comfortable fit for both sitting and standing
- For women, full skirts which allow ease of walking and an attractive drape when sitting
- Simple, uncluttered necklines that do not interfere with microphone placement

A Word about Glasses

If possible, avoid wearing glasses on camera. You may, however, wear them for two reasons: First, if people are accustomed to seeing you in glasses, they may not recognize you without glasses. Second, you may need them to read some part of your presentation or to see the person you are addressing. If you need glasses, select those with a nonglare rim, or ask the technician to use some nonglare spray on the rims. The director might ask you to tilt the glasses down just a fraction to reduce the light coming in at an angle. Although this feels clumsy to you, it looks fine to the viewers.

Eye Contact

According to independent video producer Grayson Mattingly, there are three forms of eye contact with the camera and several simple guidelines for each.

Camera as Eavesdropper

Usually you will be looking at a reporter, interviewer, or other panelists when you are on camera. This protects you from the pressure of talking directly into the impersonal lens and allows you the illusion that you are not being filmed at all. In this situation, the camera is in the role of eavesdropper. You do not need to look at the camera at all.

One caution: In an interview lasting more than a few minutes, you may very well find your interviewer turning away to talk to the floor manager or to take a sip of water while you are in the middle of speaking. In any other setting this would be a rude action indicating that you are being ignored. In a studio, however, it is all part of their responsibility. If the interviewer turns away, therefore, maintain natural eye contact with an imaginary version of him or her in the same position and location as if the interviewer were listening intently. Remember, your real audience is the thousands of viewers who are watching, not the people in the studio. Keep your poise and inner focus on that outside audience.

Camera as Listener

Have direct eye contact with the camera only when you are talking directly to the audience. Then do not look away. Look directly at the lens, and pretend that it is the eyes of the people you are addressing. Of course, you can blink, but be sure to return to the camera, the eyes of your audience. This can be tough because it is contrary to the usual speaking patterns in our culture. Usually the listener maintains eye contact while the speaker may look away, look down, or raise eyes in thought. In direct eye contact for video, those natural motions are distracting. Address the camera with your eyes.

Camera as One of the Gang

Sometimes the camera is in the studio audience or trained on the group of people to whom you are speaking. In that case, you have eye contact with the camera just as if you were an audience member. Do not focus on it, but do not shy away from brief contact.

Movement and Gestures

We close out this section on how you look on camera by considering gestures. Television studios sometimes tell guests to "sit on their hands." This advice overstates the point that television is an intimate medium. The camera picks up even the slightest nuances of face and gesture, and they convey powerful impact.

Television is not theater. Gone is the need for drama—sweeping gestures, pounding fists, and jabbing fingers. In such an intimate medium these can interfere with your message. Instead try for natural gestures. Imagine an invisible barrier 4 inches below your shoulders, and try to keep your hands below that level unless you have a particularly strong reason for being dramatic.

Reassure yourself that this small-scale and intimate quality of television makes it a powerful and potent medium for people of spirit and conviction who might never address audiences of a thousand or more.

Interview Basics

One television setting with great potential for promoting your ideas, products, or services indirectly is the interview show. You could appear on or host a local cable program or be a guest on a broadcast talk show. Your segment might run from 3 minutes to 1 hour, but the main guidelines remain the same.

Know Why You Are There

Remember the idea of magnetic marketing. Do not go on to "sell" your specific product, service, or company. Instead, position yourself as a knowledgeable and entertaining industry insider who can give the public information on how to prosper in general. Think of how you would use these general titles: "Guidelines for Investing in _____" or "Why Use Professional _____" or "Five Questions to Ask Yourself Before Selecting _____." Develop a few very specific key ideas you want to leave in the minds of your listeners, and make sure all your stories and examples relate to those key ideas. Learn to lead the interviewer gracefully back to your topic. You are being paid for your appearance only by your exposure. Maintain focus and be assured of collecting.

Extend that exposure by asking the station for a copy of the interview so that you can replay it for clients or prospects. (Station policies vary on this issue. Sometimes they ask you to bring a blank tape with you. Be sure to check on this ahead of time.)

Think Fast, Speak Briefly

Today's viewers have evolving expectations about the pacing of information. We have all—even adults—been influ-

enced by television. Yesterday's standard 60-second commercial has given way to today's 30-, 15-, and even
5-second "spot" message. Therefore keep your comments
short and clear. Whether in a 3-minute feature or 1-hour
talk show, avoid talking longer than 30 to 60 seconds at a
time. Practice becoming the 1-minute messenger, and people will be more willing to listen.

Pacing in a good interview is like a tennis match. Serves
from the interviewer should be returned crisply. Keep the
viewer's brains as active as their eyes might be in a good
match.

Involve the Audience

Always ask the audience's question—so what? What does
your information mean to them? Involve them through examples and illustrations. Spend time thinking about how a
single parent in Idaho and a heartland family in Indiana
and a polished New York financier would be affected by
the issue you are discussing. Can you give viewers any one
or two strategies that will make them healthier, safer, happier, more prosperous, more successful, more fulfilled?
Help them listen by making them feel a part of what you
say.

Concentrate on Being Visual

Brain research tells us that people listen and hear differently. Use visual aids as much as possible to appeal to
different thinking styles. Of course, slides and overhead
transparencies take time to prepare. So do not forget those
instant visual aids—your gestures, your body, and the
word pictures that your voice and words create in the
minds of your listeners.

Use precise, concrete, visual language to stir their

thoughts and emotions. For instance, compare these sentences:

1. It is a green and glowing morning brimming with promise.

2. I think it might turn out to be a nice day.

Your first response may be that sentence 1 is overly poetic. But is sentence 2 not overly boring? Do not be afraid to use rich, vivid, visual, vital language in support of your goals. Remember also that slides, props, and charts can add impact.

Say It Simply

Do you have an elderly aunt in Kansas and a sixth-grade cousin in Tennessee? If not, borrow one of each. Talk to these objective people. Pure jargon. Unless you are addressing your professional peers, as in an industry teleconference, keep your presentation elementary, basic, understandable. Sacrifice the image of erudite professional for the more challenging image of skilled communicator. Since the topic is important to you, you want your local or national community to understand and support your position.

Crisis Communication

The interview skills discussed above prepare you for the friendly interview. You also market and attract prospects by handling yourself capably in a crisis. There are three steps to good crisis communication: preparation, response, and recycling of strengths.

Preparation

Do not wait for the crisis to happen. Work now to overcome videoshock, the Walter Cronkite complex, and the slippery plateau snags. Practice the four skills outlined above in low-risk settings—*before* a crisis erupts. Schedule a thinking session once a month with yourself and perhaps your staff to ask: What are key things for our organization or industry to be proud of? What are key areas susceptible to crisis, scandal, or controversy? Note these areas on a small card, and keep it in your wallet or calendar. Rehearse some answers to imaginary hostile questions based on these issues. Be perpetually prepared to handle a crisis productively.

Response

Once a crisis erupts, follow a clear mental outline:

1. Here is the situation as we know it.
2. Here is what we are doing or trying to do.
3. Here is when we predict some results.
4. Here is a healthy perspective to take on the event.
5. Now, give us a chance to get back to solving this crisis.

This outline gives you or another spokesperson a helpful structure within which to respond. Apply this outline to some recent crisis or controversy in your field, and see how it works. Practice several times until the progression becomes natural for you. Your genuine concern, confidence, honesty, reassurance, and commitment to the best solution may protect lives and the public interest. They may also protect the productive, positive view people have of your product or industry. Remember, if people see you panic or hear tension in your voice, they assume it is your response to the situation and not just your nervousness at being interviewed. Therefore, keep the focus on the message you need to deliver, not on yourself.

Recycling Strengths

After any such challenge, sit back and consider: What did we do well? What do we need to change? How could we have been more helpful to the public, more protective of the stockholders, better prepared for the media? The best time to prepare for your next media encounter is immediately after your last one. Write down each action you wish you had done differently, and review those notes once every 2 to 3 months. Recycle your strengths to prepare for the next challenge.

Key Ideas

- Video and television are increasingly common business communication media.
- Expand your professional opportunities by being comfortable and capable on camera.
- People you admire on camera got their skills through observation and practice. You can, too.
- Increase your impact by understanding your audience and the video technology itself.
- Apply interview basics.
- Prepare now for possible crisis communication.

CHAPTER NINE

Speaking as a Marketing Tool

What Next?

Now that you are practicing and polishing all your presenting skills, how do you profit from public speaking? How do you create the highest yield from your investment of time and energy? How do you join those respected "rulers" described by Bruce Barton, former Congressman, executive, and founder of the Batten, Barton, Durstine and Osborn advertising agency?

In my library are about a thousand volumes of biography—A rough calculation indicates that more of these deal with men who have talked themselves upward than with all the scientists, writers, saints and doers combined. Talkers have always ruled. They will continue to rule . . . the smart thing is to join them.

Join these talkers by setting some goals, selecting some target audiences, and volunteering to speak. Start with your goals. Each of your presentations helps you strengthen your skills and be more prepared for opportunities that arise. Each can also help you build visibility and reputation. Make those goals as concrete as possible, and they will help keep you motivated.

A colleague of mine sailed aboard the oceanliner *Queen Elizabeth II* and was impressed that celebrities such as racing driver Jackie Stewart and journalist-curmudgeon Cleveland Amory gave lectures for the passengers. She also realized that these stars had little privacy because people recognized them everywhere. How much easier was the lot of other speakers who talked on topics such as horoscopes or star gazing at sea. These people had topics with a lot of audience appeal, presented their sessions well, and had the rest of the trip to relax and enjoy themselves in relative privacy. "That is what I want to be," said my colleague, "a lesser luminary on the *Queen Elizabeth II*." She gave herself 10 years to polish her skills and to position herself as enough of an authority to appeal to the Cunard line. Her desire to work on one cruise every year or two fueled her efforts. She made this vow 9 years ago and has so far worked aboard the *S. S. Norway* and is still aiming for the *Queen Elizabeth II*. This concrete goal kept her working at her part-time hobby of public speaking. To what specific audience, topic, and location would you like your skills to carry you in 10 years?

Choosing the Right Audience

Whatever your goal, the right audiences can help you reach it. Although any audience gives you the opportunity to practice your skills, a carefully selected group can give you much more. The best audience would be one filled with decision makers in need of your product, service, or idea, sitting there with cash in their hands and intending to go back to the office with whatever you are offering. Never have I seen such an audience, but that does not stop me from seeking one. Barring that ideal group, the next best audience includes some members pleasantly close to that description.

Find your best audience by asking yourself some questions:

- Where, geographically, do I want to have visibility and credibility? Do I need it in my neighborhood, community, the nearest metropolitan area, the state, the region, the country, the world?

- Who are my best prospects or the people who influence those prospects? Should I be talking to executives, school children, travel agents, engineers, teachers, attorneys, senior citizens, church groups, service organizations, shift workers? If the primary target group is hard to reach, can I get through to someone who influences them?

- What kinds of gatherings do these people attend? Do they have monthly luncheons, quarterly educational programs, special seminars, ice cream socials?

- What kinds of topics do they want to hear about? Can my information make them healthier, wealthier, safer, more popular, happier, more challenged? Is there a logical match between something they might want to hear about and the impression I want to leave of me, my organization, my services?

- What level of response from them will have made my investment of time and attention pay off appropriately? Have they responded that way in the past to other speakers? Are they likely to respond that way to me? Are there steps the program planner can take to help ensure this response? Are there steps I need to take?

Once you have answered those questions, you should have a clear focus on your prime audiences. Chances are that you are already a member of some professional or industry groups you may want to address. Why not start there? Call the program chair of your organizations and volunteer. Some people hesitate to do this. "That room will be packed with my competitors," they complain. It will also be packed with people whose respect and connections can advance your goals.

Find out when the next regional and national conference is. Volunteer again—even if it means filling out a proposal form. Such participation can bring you an invaluable and extensive network of colleagues and even some clients.

Do not stop there. Too many professionals mix only with others in their own industry. Ask yourself where your clients or prospects are. What groups do they belong to? Can you volunteer for those groups? Decide now on six groups you will contact. Check your telephone book to find names of organizations you probably never knew existed. Here are a few to get you started thinking:

Chamber of Commerce
Board of Trade
American Business Womens Association
American Society of Association Executives
American Society for Training and Development
The Democratic or Republican Club
Religious or church groups
Business and Professional Women's Club
International Association of Business Communicators
Historical Society

Elks
Moose
Kiwanis
Rotary
United Way
American Association of Retired People
Senior citizens' groups
Hospitals
Colleges and universities
Bridge clubs
Travel clubs
Parents Without Partners
Singles' clubs
Athletic or health clubs

Once you have selected a few groups to contact, focus on some topics crafted to capture their interest and respect. Get in touch with the program planner. Here is a sample letter you might use to offer your presentation:

Dear _____ :

Can I be of help to you in planning one of your group's programs? I would be pleased to do a session for you on one of my most requested topics:

- Never Play Leapfrog with Unicorns: The Guide to Managing Your Risks
- Retroactive Fire Insurance: Creativity and the Bottom Line
- Using the Whole in Your Head: Thinking Styles and Strategies for the Whole Brain

These and other topics relating to personal and professional productivity could be tailored for your group.

Each of the sessions is designed to give the group concrete guidelines and practical tips based on my 12 years of business experience. I have presented these programs to business and community groups with good success. Feel free to call me at (202) 202-0202 for more information and the names of my references.

Cordially,

_____

You may want to follow up your letter with a call a few days later. If the planner is interested and you decide to do the program, ask for some recent copies of their newsletter and other information which will help you know your audience. Again, the checklist in Chapter 4 will help you plan. If the planner is interested but the program calendar is full, ask to stay in the file for next year's schedule or offer to be available as an emergency fill-in if another speaker should cancel. If the planner is not interested, move on to another target group. In any case, you may want to contact next year's program committee and be considered again.

Choosing Your Topic

Consider the paradox: Nobody wants to listen to you deliver a commercial for your business as your speech, yet you want to speak as a way of promoting that very business. How do you handle this dilemma? Subtly. The first rule to recognize in choosing your topic is that it must be generic and valuable while still being a subtle commercial. Respect the fact that standing there in front of them is already a powerful commercial, and giving them a handout or novelty item with your name and address is another. Within a 30-minute presentation, you should spend no more than 30 seconds mentioning your company. You can, of course, reinforce your main points with illustrations featuring your experiences. But judge this carefully. Audiences can be resistant or even angry if you are too commercial. Indeed, you will often win great respect by asking your introducer to announce the name of your company and not mentioning it yourself at all.

What are *generic* topics? They are topics which inform listeners about an era or industry without specifically featuring your organization. A generic topic builds demand for the products and services of your competitor at the same time as it builds demand for yours. Theoretically, generic topics create a bigger pie for all to share in. The fact that you are the person whom this audience has come to respect, however, significantly improves your position in the minds of these listeners. Here are some idea starters for producing your own list of generic topics. Notice that these are not yet speech titles: they are the content focus of your talk:

How to . . .

How to prosper in the coming . . .

How to guarantee your family's . . .

Commonsense solutions to . . .

Three steps to . . .
Why do you need a professional . . .
Getting control of . . .
Thirty days to a more powerful . . .
Building effective . . .
Secrets of . . .
Strategies for success in . . .
. . . is for you!
Lessons from the history of . . .
Ten minutes a day to . . .
View from the top: Secrets of successful . . .
Celebrity stories: My most unforgettable . . .
The five biggest mistakes . . . make
Building tomorrow's headlines in . . .
Essentials of . . .
Basic . . .
Learning to improve your . . .
What to do when you get your hands on . . .
Advice to a . . .
The dangers of . . .
. . . can change your life
Laughter, stress, and . . .

Pick five of the idea starters, and convert them to topics you could offer. Juggle several until you have some that would appeal to audiences and would be consistent with subtle promotion on your part. Here are a few, for example, which would be appropriate for someone involved in travel or conference planning:

- Hassle-free packing
- Why use a professional travel agent?
- Food choices for travelers
- Staying fit on the road
- Travel safety and security

These would be appropriate for accountants or financial planners:

- Understanding the new tax laws
- Banking deregulation and your dollars
- Do I really need a will?
- Understanding the financial puzzle
- Secrets of profitable investing

These would be appropriate for someone in supervision, training, or human resource management:

- America's neglected resource—employees
- Painless performance appraisal
- Supervising baby-boom employees
- Secrets of successful staffing
- Dos, don'ts, and maybes of the hiring interview

Truth in Titling

The title of your presentation should do two things: It should intrigue people enough to attend, and it should describe the topic accurately. A title such as "Taxes" is too general. "Opportunities from Oppression" may intrigue you, but it does not specify the topic. "Opportunities from Oppression: How to Profit from Today's Changing Tax Environment" is a title that both intrigues and describes. Titles of 5 to 15 words are appropriate for speeches. These long titles help people decide whether to invest their time listening to you. If your speech is competing with several concurrent activities, the title helps ensure that people select wisely. One formula that works well is to start with a catchy or concrete slogan or phrase, insert a colon, and describe the subject accurately after the colon. Here are a few examples:

- Anchovies to Zucchini: The Role of Nutrition in Your Fitness Plan

- Senior Safari: Action and Adventure Await Retired Travelers
- The Medium Is the Madness: Your Role in Directing the Future of Television
- When Last Liberty Smiled: The Evolving Challenge of Immigration
- Starring *You:* Preparing for Your Media Debut

Here are some additional examples linked to groups you might target:

Group	Setting	Title or Topic
Engineers	Monthly professional meeting	Stop Watching TV by Candlelight: How to Computerize Your Project Management
Outside sales force	Quarterly regional training session	Turbocharge Your Elephant: Harnessing Client Objections to Speed the Sale
Trade Association	International conference	Do It with Chopsticks: Mastering the Finer Points of International Negotiations
Hospital professionals	Nationwide teleconference	What to Do When Everybody's Pushing the Panic Button: Dealing Intelligently with Epidemics
College administrators	Planning retreat	The Marketing Maze: Commonsense Solutions to Marketing Higher Education
Employees and spouses	Resort Convention	Seesaws, Sandboxes, and Samsonite: Balancing Your Personal and Professional Life

Magnetic Marketing

This, then, is the goal of your presentation: to create a niche in the minds of clients or prospects so that when a product or service is needed, yours is the first name that comes to mind and no substitute is considered suitable. You win their respect, their contracts or business, and eventually their hearts because people love doing business with true professionals. Each of your presentations builds toward mastery—mastery of your skills and mastery of your market. "Mastery," philosopher John Gardner said, "is not something that strikes in an instant, like a thunderbolt, but a gathering power that moves steadily through time, like weather." Become weather, not the thunderbolt.

In planning the content of your magnetic marketing presentation, you will probably use the persuasive outline from Chapter 5, blending information and inspiration. Here is a sample opening of such a presentation used by film producer Dana Balibrera.

Winners All Our Lives: Fun and Fitness Over Fifty

There is a scene in the Wizard of Oz *where the Wizard turns to the Cowardly Lion and says, "Take your fortitude and parade it down the street." It almost seems as if thousands of us have been listening, for the amazing and heartening fact is that fitness over fifty is becoming a reality. Fortitude is fighting the rocking chair. Senior America is parading it down the street. Not only parading, they are also staging the Masters Games—Olympics for Seniors. As a recent witness to the masters games in Puerto Rico, I'm here today with three messages for you—no matter what your age. First, endurance, stamina, fitness, and vitality are qualities you can nurture all your lives. Second, setting goals and working gradually toward them over time can yield startling results. (Just ask our award-winning runner who started at age 65!) Third, as senior citizens form an increasingly large portion of our population (and perhaps our market), it is important to move beyond old stereotypes and recognize new, energetic realities.*

Dana Balibrera closed with these thoughts:

Former President Dwight D. Eisenhower said, "I'm saving that rocker for the day when I feel as old as I really am." Join the energetic Eisenhower; join the paraders of fortitude. Put these three ideas to work in your life:
* *Attend to your fitness no matter how young or old you are.*

* *Set goals you can work at patiently over time.*

* *Recognize and respect the tremendous resource of senior citizens.*

When you look in your own mirror tomorrow morning in the privacy of your own bathroom, imagine your face at 40, at 20, at 80. See the places it was going, the place it is going, and the place it is now. Be kind to that container. It is the packaging of your entire history, your entire potential. Unto this awareness, I commend us all.

Notice how commercial-free Balibrera's presentation is. She had arranged with the introducer to mention before and after the session that she works with people in the areas of fitness and goal setting.

Multiplying Your Impact

How can you ensure that you get the most benefit from
your presentation? Here are some possibilities:

- If you ever hope to hear from any of these people
  again, they need to have your name, address, and
  phone number to contact you. One easy way to do this
  is to have a one-page handout on your company letter-
  head that reviews the three key ideas of your presentation. Give this out at the end of your session. An alternative is to have a novelty item, a free ballpoint pen or
  calendar, with your name and number. Try to ensure
  they can contact you if they want to.

- Ask the program planner if there is a list of those attending or a directory of their membership. This could
  become your list for a follow-up mailing on some issue
  related to your topic. In such a mailing, it is usually
  appropriate to ask for the person's business. If in
  doubt, ask the program planner. If no list is available
  or if they do not give them away, you can consider offering a door prize to anyone who gives you a business
  card or just their name and address on a piece of paper.
  Have an audience member draw a winner for you, and
  give that winner an inexpensive gift or some product or
  service offered by your company. You can then keep
  the cards as a mailing list.

- Invite a client or prospect to the speech as your special
  guest. Who is the decision maker or the assistant to
  that decision maker that you might invite? Think of
  one or two people you are trying to impress. They are
  not members of the group you are addressing, so they
  would not ordinarily know about your speech. When
  you issue such an invitation, you let them know you
  are developing into more of a recognized "name" in
  this area; you flatter them by your invitation and
  thereby become more memorable to them. They might
  even attend. If they express interest but cannot attend,
  offer to send them an audiotape of the session. Such
  small attentions are potent marketing techniques.

- Invite the program planner to audiotape or videotape the session and provide you with a complimentary review copy. If she or he does not exercise this option, do it yourself. Get an inexpensive tape dubber, and make duplicate copies of your speech to send to appropriate prospects, just as you might send them an interesting article you ran across. Also remember, videotape equipment can be set up in the back of the room and left untended during your session. You do not get back the most dramatic product, but you do get a realistic record of your session.

- Also invite press coverage. If you can hook into today's news or big issues, you might attract the attention of the metropolitan press. Remember the geographic area to which you are trying to sell. If you want to make a big name right in your community, the local press may be easier to reach and may be more inclined to give you coverage.

- Does the group take photographs? Tell them you would be pleased for their photographer to catch you in action and for them to give you a copy of the prints, preferably black and white.

- Why not turn the speech content into an article? The group you are addressing could use it in their magazine and could submit it to their industry's national magazine. You could offer the article to newspapers or magazines that your prospects might read. You need not get paid for the article if it is likely to bring in business. If you like the idea of the article but you hate to write, give your audiotape to a ghostwriter and let a professional polish your prose. Many cities have writers' groups and talented professionals who charge $15 to $45 an hour. Working with a ghostwriter is perfectly ethical and is standard business practice. Yours is the only name listed as author in such arrangements.

- Consider bringing your own camera. People love to receive photographs of themselves in the mail. Have your camera with you at these events—one which is simple and easy to operate and takes excellent pictures. Either you can take pictures of people you want to follow up, or you can draft someone to photograph you with this prospect. Send the pictures along later with a note. Be remembered.

Put these ideas to work for you. They can help your magnetic marketing build your visibility. They can help you move away from marketing with a butterfly net, where you have to go out and capture each new prospect and drag him or her in, kicking and screaming. Magnetic marketing repositions you as the person whose visibility attracts the kind of clients and business you want.

They Offered to Pay You?

The real payoff to a magnetic marketing presentation is the increase in your business. In some cases, though, your presentations become so polished and so popular that you are sought after as a speaker. More than a few well-earning professional speakers started their careers when they realized that speaking not only enhanced their main ambition—it became that ambition. Such a transition sometimes happens gradually, sometimes quickly. Just to help you recognize the signposts along the way, here are seven stages of speaking—from the $25 fee to the $50,000 fee.

The Candle

At this stage the planner offers you a $25 to $100 honorarium. Of course, you do not have to pay for the lunch, and they may even throw in a free sweatshirt with the club logo on it. Although the money here is nice and would pay for your gas and parking, you may get more marketing impact if you donate it to the organization's foundation or pet project.

The Lightbulb

Here you are offered, or request, $100 to $250 if that is appropriate for the organization's budget. You are investing considerable time in preparing and delivering your speech, and this is reasonable compensation. At this event you may be given a coffee mug or paperweight decorated with their logo.

The Spotlight

Now your fees range from $250 to $750. You are seen as a hometown celebrity, someone developing a name but still interchangeable with others who could speak on the same topic. Your souvenir here is likely to be a certificate of appreciation (unframed).

The Beacon

Your light shines farther afield. You are beginning to be seen as a significant emerging professional. Your fees are in the $750 to $1500 range plus expenses since you are traveling more. You still do some programs on a complimentary basis for special causes or to market your services to highly desirable clients. At this level you might receive a travel clock as a thank-you gift.

The Star

You are now established as a respected name in your field. Your fees range from $1500 to $5000 per program, and clients feel lucky to find an open slot on your calendar that matches their convention dates. Your memento here might be something tasteful in leather—a frame, notebook, or traveling office kit.

The Superstar

You are now definitely in the celebrity ranks. Your name and photograph appear in national publications. Although you are not a world leader or a major entertainment personality, your name is recognized. When they notice your name in the program, some people will come especially to see or hear you. At this level your fees range $5000 to $10,000, and you are treated to a suite with flowers or a wine and cheese tray.

The Nova

You are now a big name of the day. News of your presentation is featured in conference publicity, and your stature draws an additional 1200 registrations (and their fees). People hardly care what you talk about—they want to breathe the same air you do for an hour or so. They want to see and hear you in person. They want to brag about seeing you when they get back home. The good news for novas is that they can earn $10,000 to $50,000 per program plus first-class air fare and a chauffeured limosine. The tough news is that your nova period is brief. As the dictionary says, a nova is "a star which suddenly increases its brightness and energy enormously, then fades into its former obscurity." Your nova status reflects your position at a point in history more than it does your presenting skills. If those skills are substantial, you can retreat with dignity back to superstar status.

Notice that in the first three stages, your topic and its value and relevance for the audience are the prime factors. In the next two stages people come for your personal perspective and views on the topic. In the final two stages, your topic may be incidental. They are coming for *you*.

If public speaking does become more than a business skill or hobby for you, investigate the benefits of joining the National Speakers Association. This professional society supports the development of speaking professionals at all levels from part time to full time. Their local chapters, regional workshops, annual conventions, and other services offer you current, practical, and profitable strategies for success. Their directory is distributed to members and meeting planners across the country and around the world. Here is a sampling of the topics at this year's convention in Phoenix, Arizona.

- Developing a Salable Talk
- Effective Listening: A Critical Skill for Successful Speakers
- Becoming the Meeting Planner's Partner
- How to Design and Conduct a Seminar
- How to Give the Best Speech of Your Life—Every Time
- Building a Secure Financial Tomorrow . . . Today
- Put Your Money Where Your Mouth Is
- Internationally Speaking
- The Speaking Business: Soup to Nuts and Bolts
- Who Is Hiring Whom . . . and Why
- The Road Warrior—Surviving on the Road
- Get Up Off Your Assets

To find out more, contact:

NATIONAL SPEAKERS ASSOCIATION
4747 North Seventh Street, Suite 310
Phoenix, Arizona 85014
(602) 265-1001

In your quest for the $50,000 fees, never lose sight of the fact that for most people the value of magnetic marketing is that it generates interest and income in the field, profession, or business they practice for their entire career. While nova status appeals to our dimly remembered childhood fantasies of becoming movie starts, sports celebrities, ballerinas, or rock stars, successful speaking and magnetic marketing can and do serve you all the days of your life.

Afterword

E. B. White wrote an essay years ago called "The Second Tree from the Corner" (E. B. White, *The Second Tree from the Corner*, Harper & Row, New York, 1984). In it he told a brief story about Trexler, a modern urban everyman. Trexler visited his psychiatrist over a period of time, hoping to understand an undefined yearning inside himself, hoping at last to recognize what he wanted out of life. After one late-afternoon session, Trexler walked out of his doctor's building into Central Park on an evening of clearing weather. As he walked, he recognized that he was vaguely pleased that what he wanted was impossible to describe, that it was deep, formless, and enduring. He was pleased that it was not a boat, a car, a wing on his house—but something impossible to fulfill. He felt invigorated.

Suddenly his sickness seemed health, his dizziness stability. A small tree, rising between him and the light stood there, saturated with the evening, each gilt-edged leaf perfectly drunk with excellence and delicacy . . . . "I want the second tree from the corner just as it stands," answering an imaginary question from an imaginary physician. And he felt a slow pride in realizing that what he wanted none could bestow, and that what he had, none could take away.

We are like Trexler in our yearning to be more capable communicators. We are not always sure what outcome we want or what skills we need to develop. Sometimes, though, we see that tree, "saturated with the evening." Sometimes we read a passage or hear a speaker whose gild-edged words are "perfectly drunk with excellence and delicacy." Savor such moments. Plant them in your brain. Let them yield a forest of models. Visit your models often. Keep asking yourself, "What do I really want from communicating?" Once you have answered that question, go back to your forest of models and find out what that purpose looks like in the hands of masters. How can you grow into similar mastery?

This book opened with comments on the challenges you face and closes with a focus on mastery. The quest is demanding, but there may not be another professional journey more worth making. Godspeed!

Appendix I

PRESENTATION PLANNING SHEET

1. Topic:

2. Date to Present:

3. Location:

4. Time Allowed/Needed

5. What Do I Want to Accomplish?

6. What Are the Important Factors in the Idea, Program,
    Product I Am Describing?

7. How Will It Benefit These Listeners?

8. What Response/Follow-Through Am I Seeking from Them?

9. What Style of Presentation Is Likely to Be Most Effective?
   Level of detail
   Level of formality
   Level of language (technical or general)
   Pattern of organization

10. What Resources Will I Use or Quote From?

11. What Visuals or Props Support the Presentation?

12. What Audience Involvement Might Be Appropriate?

13. How Will I Structure or Observe Their Follow-Through

14. How Will I Know the Presentation Was a Success?

Preliminary Notes or Outline

Appendix II

PRESENTATION POWER CHECKLIST

This form helps you evaluate others or coach yourself. Review live presentations, audiotapes, or videotapes of a specific speech. Make notes according to this scale:

$$4 = \text{Excellent}$$
$$3 = \text{Good}$$
$$2 = \text{Acceptable, average}$$
$$1 = \text{Needs work}$$
$$0 = \text{Does not apply}$$

SPEAKER: DATE:

AUDIENCE: SUBJECT:

PROGRAM PURPOSE: REVIEWER/OBSERVER:

WORDS AND STRUCTURE:

_____ Appropriate to subject

_____ Appropriate to audience

_____ Appropriate to theme/event

_____ Appropriate length

_____ Effective opening

_____ Clear development

_____ Instigated appropriate action

_____ Avoided jargon

_____ Used lively, powerful language

_____ Supported key points

_____ Avoided nonwords (Um . . .)

_____ Powerful closing

COMMENTS:

VOICE:

_____ Pitch	_____ Projection
_____ Rate	_____ Breath support
_____ Variety	_____ Expressed confidence
_____ Articulation	_____ Expressed sincerity

COMMENTS:

NONVERBAL:

_____ Room geography	_____ General appearance
_____ Clothing	_____ Eye contact
_____ Gestures	_____ Pauses for poise
_____ Stance	_____ Pauses for impact

COMMENTS:

TECHNICAL AIDS:

_____ Lectern	_____ Slides
_____ Microphone	_____ Film/video/music
_____ Overhead	_____ Props

COMMENTS:

GENERAL IMPACT OF PRESENTATION:

MAJOR STRENGTHS:

AREAS FOR DEVELOPMENT:

Index